Altwerger and Mandel Publishing Co., Inc.
6346 Orchard Lake Road, Suite 201
West Bloomfield, Michigan 48322
© 1992 by James Clary

Printed in the United States of America

ISBN 1-878005-72-3-Pb
ISBN 1-878005-46-4-Cl

Limited edition, signed and numbered collector prints of the J. Clary paintings in this book can be obtained by contacting:

Cap'n Jim's Gallery
201 N. Riverside
St. Clair, MI 48079
313-329-7744

BY JAMES CLARY

A&M
Altwerger and Mandel Publishing Company
West Bloomfield, Michigan

Altwerger and Mandel Publishing Co., Inc.
6346 Orchard Lake Road, Suite 201
West Bloomfield, Michigan 48322
© 1992 by James Clary

Printed in the United States of America

ISBN 1-878005-46-4

Limited edition, signed and numbered collector prints of the J. Clary paintings in this book can be obtained by contacting:

Cap'n Jim's Gallery
201 N. Riverside
St. Clair, MI 48079
313-329-7744

To my late father who
instilled me with the
dream that if you only
apply yourself, you can
be anything you want to
be.

Contents

Preface

Long before my career as a marine artist began, I realized the lack of readily available information on many of the historic and nostalgic ships of the Great Lakes, both pictorial and in literature. Not then having access to the information in marine museums, I discovered how difficult it was for the average person, not acquainted with any historical institution, to acquire this knowledge. A true gap existed between the accessible museum data and the material at the fingertips of the interested party. About the same time, my personal interest in Great Lakes lore exploded. Diving headlong into this fascinating research, I found that many others were also yearning for a glimpse at the maritime past that was seemingly lost or buried.

Not trying necessarily to fill this gap, I began work on a few selected Great Lakes vessels through the help of the late Robert E. Lee, former curator of the Dossin Great Lakes Museum in Detroit. When merely ankle deep into the first project (*Tashmoo: Ladies of the Lakes I*), the idea of an entire series came to mind, and the work on these subjects began under the name of Great Lakes History in Art. Lithograph prints were made from the original paintings and sold through dealers and galleries.

During the research for each painting, I collected documents, photographs, and other artifacts from each ship. Together with these treasures and many interesting facts about each vessel, I felt that after my painting project was completed, it would be a shame not to share this information. Thus, this book, the continuation of *Ladies of the Lakes I*, was in the making long ago. Here, then, is a digest of information on selected subjects in the Great Lakes series now a part of the Maritime History in Art.

J. Clary

Acknowledgments

Grateful acknowledgment is made to the following persons and institutions for their assistance in the authentication of the *Ladies of the Lakes II* paintings and historical text: Dossin Great Lakes Museum, Belle Isle, Detroit; the Great Lakes Historical Society, Vermilion, Ohio; the Burton Collection, Detroit Public Library, Detroit; the United States Coast Guard Museum, United States Coast Guard Academy, New London; the Ninth Coast Guard District, Cleveland; Pilot House Museum, Corunna, Ontario; Lambton County Library, Wyoming, Ontario; Sarnia Public Library, Sarnia, Ontario; James O'Carroll, Donald Stobbe, and J. H. LeCompte, Bethlehem Steel, Great Lakes Steamship Division; the United States Naval Institute, Annapolis; Archives of the United States; Library of Congress, Washington, D.C.; NBC Audience Services, New York City; Bob Lawson, Tailhook Association, Benita, California; Project Lightship, a nonprofit division of the Museum of Arts and History, Port Huron, Michigan; the Collingwood Museum, Collingwood, Ontario; the Collingwood Library, Collingwood, Ontario; and the Huron County Goderich Museum, Goderich, Ontario; Lorain Public Library, Lorain, Ohio; the Great Lakes Shipwreck Historical Society, Sault Ste. Marie, Michigan; Manistee Historical Museum, Manistee, Michigan; Milwaukee Public Library, marine collection, Milwaukee; Mal Sillars and Paul Gross, WDIV-TV, Detroit meteorologists; the late Adm. Edwin Roland, USCG (Ret); Adm. Richard Schmidtman, USCG (Ret); Capt. Gordon Hall, USCG; Capt. F. J. Honke, USCG; Comdr. John Bannan, USCG; Capt. Clifford MacLean, USCG (Ret); Capt. Gilbert F. Schumacher, USCG (Ret); BM2 William Garrett, USCG; Nelson Zimmer, naval architect, and Raymond Assel, oceanographer, U. S. Dept. of Commerce, Great Lakes Environmental Research Laboratory, Ann Arbor, Michigan; Mr. and Mrs. Ralph Yates, Mr. and the late Mrs. Paul Hurt, Robert C. Burchill, Gene Onchulenko, Don More, Dr. Robert Clifford, Dr. W. M. Taylor, Marguerite Seguin, Betty Webb, Betty Ann Conley, Rose Starkweather, Virginia Lossing, Marcea Thoms, Doris Smith, Mr. Boughner, Winifred Richmond, Roland Anderson, Lucille Fennert, Jenny Sickle, Gladys Thompson, Mimie Lanton, Malcolm McRae, Mr. and

Mrs. James Pulcher and group of five, Skip Neff and group of two, Norma Liner, Mr. and Mrs. John McKinley, Margaret Hyde, Mr. and Mrs. Harold Cook, Mrs. Norman Cristick, Alan Anderson, Capt. A. Sparling, Bill Lindsay, Mr. and Mrs. G. Guyor and group of two, John Brown, Mr. and Mrs. Ernie Slipp, John McKay, Jim Cassin and two bellboys, Mrs. Pemberton Page, Mr. and Mrs. Buntebart, Mrs. R. E. Harneck, Mr. and Mrs. Martin, Mr. and Mrs. Laird Nixon, Mr. and Mrs. D. R. Wilson and group of two, Mrs. Howard M. Clark and group of two, Mr. Isaacs, Mrs. Grace Scott and group of three, R. E. Campbell, Mr. and Mrs. Stanley McDonald, Antholl Murray, Capt. William Taylor, Capt. Bob Brabander, John Presley, John Guba, historian; R. A. Chick Eldridge, Marlene Porter, William Patterson, diver; Edward Kanaby, Wayne Brusate, and Paul Schmitt, divers; Richard T. Race, president, Hydrograpic Survey Co., Chicago; David Trotter, Undersea Research Associates, Canton, Michigan; G. Kent Bellrichard, diver; Mike Van Hoey, lighthouse historian; Richard Bennett, diver; Irene Dundas, Mary Rose, and the late Joyce Callahan.

1. THE *MACKINAW*

She's ready to help in the hour of need,
To break some blue or do a good deed.
Windrows of thirty they say she'll crack,
No job is too big for the mighty Mac.

Even though unnavigable ice on Great Lakes waters was, on the average, no more severe than in other high latitudes, the pioneering spirit and inspiration of our Great Lakes sailors and naval architects made possible the ice-breaking technology that we know today. What is believed to be one of the earliest ice-breaking vessels was the steam packet *Chief Justice Robinson*, built at Niagara in upper Canada in 1842. Though not built specifically as an ice-breaking vessel, this 160-foot passenger steamer had an unusual protruding prow that allowed the vessel to break ice from underneath. The odd look of this protrusion was like the bulbous addition on the bows of many of today's vessels.

Countless stories abound of the tiny tugs and tireless crews that fought the mountains of ice to keep channels and harbors open on the Great Lakes during the days before the big "ice crushers." One such "little giant" was the tug W. L. *Mercereau*, which operated out of Chicago. Old-timers said that she would go hopping along on the tough ice, almost out of the water, to bounce into an opening and crush a path for helpless ships.

A review of a few old weather records will bring into focus the monumental ice obstacles that confronted these sailors. Long periods of severe cold and gale winds that shifted and stacked ice into giant windrows stopped many a vessel and held them in frozen jaws. The great ice blockade in the Straits of Mackinac in 1922, for example, produced walls of windrowed ice so impenetrable that the strongest ice crushers of the time could not break through the barrier. For a record, a virtual mountain chain of ice was created off Mackinac Point in 1939 when the height of windrowed ice reached fifty-seven feet. Weather systems also produced freak consequences of unusual dimension. In December

With its bulbous bow protrusion, the *Chief Justice Robinson* is believed to be one of the earliest configurations of an ice-breaking vessel. (Chicago Historical Society; sketch, steamer *Chief Justice Robinson*, from a sketch by Capt. Jas Van Cleve in 1843)

The "little giant" tug *W. L. Mercereau*, which operated out of Chicago as an early icebreaker before the days of the big "ice crushers."

The *Mackinaw*

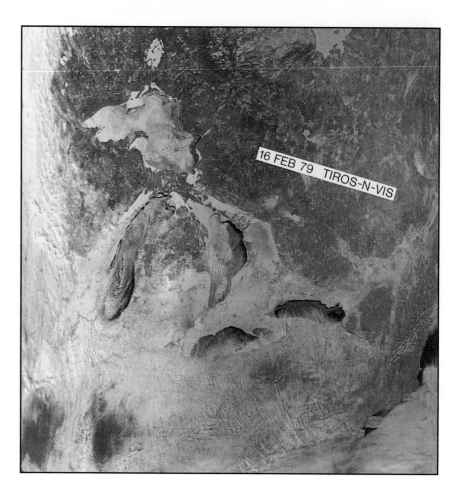

Satellite photograph taken during the winter of 1978-79, when, for the first time in recorded history, all the Great Lakes completely froze over at one time. (Great Lakes Environmental Research Laboratory)

1926, when 140 steamers were locked in the ice of the St. Marys River due to a sudden cold wave, it was feared that the ships would be held there until the spring thaw. The weather moderated overnight, however, and the imprisoned vessels were free in a few days. More recently in 1972, ice remained intact in western Lake Superior until June, and during the winter of 1978-79 when, for the first time in recorded history, all the Great Lakes completely froze over.

In early days of sail, when the movement of goods was no less important than today, as the door of winter closed, all ship traffic ceased until the spring, and that was that. Before 1880, with no railroad lines running north other than from Chicago, with steamers running only during the navigation season, vast areas of the northern states, especially the Upper Peninsula of Michigan, were virtually cut off from the lower areas. Fortunately, with the wider use of steam and more powerful vessels, the outright increased demand for goods brought about an ardent obsession not only to lengthen the navigation season on both ends, winter and spring, but also to try to run through the winter.

So in 1887, when the Mackinac Transportation Company

(MTC) ordered the ferry *St. Ignace* from the Detroit Dry Dock Company, the art of ice breaking took one giant leap. Realizing the acute need for a ferry to operate in the Straits of Mackinac, the company secured the services of the well-known designer, Frank E. Kirby, who had been consulting with Capt. L. R. Boynton of the steamer *Algomah*. Captain Boynton, along with his expertise in navigating vessels in heavy ice, was said to have first envisioned the bow propeller. Locked in the ice off Alpena Harbor during the winter of 1872-73, Boynton was sure he could have freed his vessel if he had a propeller forward as well as aft. From this vision, the idea and design of the bow propeller came to be.

The *St. Ignace*, fitted with this first bow propeller and a spoon-shaped prow that enabled the vessel to rise up on ice, was the pioneer prototype icebreaker, whose design would be duplicated and improved in the years to come. Her trim tanks for leveling unequal loads permitted lateral motion to free the vessel in heavy ice. In testimony of her unique and practical design, during her maiden trip north from Detroit in April 1888, she made a steady five miles per hour in ice two feet thick for most of her trip.

Although the *St. Ignace* proved herself well as an ice-breaker far above the capability of any of her earlier and smaller counterparts, she was too small, and so another ferry, the *Sainte Marie I*, was added to the service in 1893. She also had a bow propeller, but unlike the *St. Ignace*, she had an oak, steel-sheathed, double hull and four smokestacks. She could plunge through ice twenty-seven inches thick and

The pioneer icebreaker and car ferry, the *St. Ignace*, which was fitted with the first bow propeller. (Great Lakes Historical Society)

was thought to be the heaviest hull on the Great Lakes at the time. So renowned were the feats of these two vessels that Russian naval officials came to St. Ignace, Michigan, to witness their ice-breaking abilities. The Russians later had a steamer built in England based on the design of the *Sainte Marie I*. They later dismantled the vessel and had it reconstructed for use in Siberia.

The *Chief Wawatam* joined the MTC in 1911 and the *Sainte Marie II* followed in 1913. These two ferries had steel hulls and were also designed by Frank Kirby. The bow propellers and the unique hulls of these four vessels were instrumental in the design of an icebreaker desperately needed by the United States Coast Guard on the Great Lakes during World War II. With all of the available cutters, including the 165-foot icebreakers *Escanaba* and *Tahoma*, called to war service on the Atlantic, not a single icebreaker was available for duty on the Great Lakes even though a major push for war materials demanded a longer navigation season. Because of this acute need, on December 17, 1941, the Third Supplemental National Defense Appropriation Act provided $10 million for the construction of an icebreaker especially for Great Lakes use. Designed by the naval architectural firm of Gibbs and Cox and developed as a byproduct of the "wind" class icebreakers *Northwind I*, *Eastwind*, *Southwind*, and *Westwind*, this special vessel would include all previous icebreaker-design characteristics adapted from the *St. Ignace*, *Sainte Marie I* and *II*, the *Chief Wawatam*, and the Swedish icebreaker *Ymer*, besides many modern innovative features. Known at first as the *Manitowoc*, the name was later changed to *Mackinaw* as the navy had already assigned *Manitowoc* to a patrol frigate. Although she would be much like the "wind" class vessels, which had a 269-foot length and a 63$\frac{1}{2}$-foot beam, it was said that the *Mackinaw* was nothing but a "wind" class ship that was squashed down, pushed out, and extended to meet Great Lakes requirements.

Her keel was laid March 20, 1943, at the Toledo Shipbuilding Company, but practically everything built around the keel fell outside the boundaries of shipbuilding tradition. Perhaps the most unusual feat of construction was her extremely strong hull. The 1$\frac{5}{8}$" mild steel hull plating contained no rivets, and her frames, spaced sixteen inches apart, made a truss configuration similar to what might be found in an inverted gymnasium. An inner shell was then placed inside these trusses; the area between the inner and outer plating was divided into many tanks that were to be used for fuel and ballast for heeling. She would have an

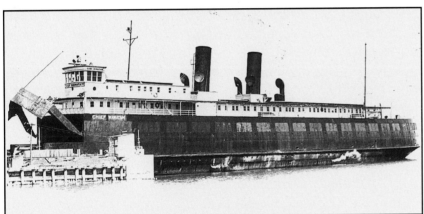

The car ferry *Sainte Marie* had a bow propeller, an oak, steel-sheathed double hull, and four smokestacks. (Dossin Great Lakes Museum)

Another pioneer icebreaker, the venerable car ferry *Chief Wawatam*, which was scrapped in 1989. (Great Lakes Historical Society)

The car ferry *Chief Wawatam*, working through stacks of windrowed ice.

The icebreaker *Mackinaw*, in dry dock revealing her bow propeller.

overall length of 290 feet, a beam of 74′ 5″, and a displacement of 5,090 tons—a tremendous weight for that size vessel. Hailed as the most powerful icebreaker in the world, each of her six diesel engines would produce two thousand horsepower. She would be capable of making 18.7 miles per-hour and would be driven by two fourteen-foot-diameter propellers.

The monstrous task of shaping her extra thick hull plates was one reason for her great cost, and the method of forming some of these plates, though not unusual in shipbuilding, still was almost primitive in concept. Nelson Zimmer, a naval architect, worked at the shipyard during the building of the *Mackinaw*; he recalls that the propeller shaft boss plating was heated and pulled from the furnace "limp." This white-hot 1⁵/₈″ plate was laid over a skeleton form made according to the inside shape of the boss. Four men then hammered the plate to the shape of this form with a huge rammer, made so that all four men could hammer in unison. It was old-time shipwright ingenuity at work on a modern vessel.

As with her earlier counterparts, she was fitted with a twelve-foot bow propeller, but unique to the *Mackinaw* was a notch built into her stern. It was fashioned so that the bow of a vessel under tow could be lashed into this slot so that both vessels could move as one. Heeling and trimming tanks were another feature that would later free her from heavy ice. Thirty-inch transfer pipes allowed tons of water to move fore and aft or side to side in minutes to produce the rocking

20

or rolling necessary to better break ice.

When completion delays led to severe penalties that resulted in the bankruptcy of the Toledo Shipbuilding Company, the contract for the *Mackinaw* was taken over by the American Shipbuilding Company, who expedited and completed the project. Soon, the launching date was set for March 4, 1944. A phrase often heard to describe this vessel taking shape in the yard was "the unique *Mackinaw*," and her launching, too, was certainly unique. Nelson Zimmer was asked to prepare a launch calculation to help reckon with just how this seventy-five-foot beamed vessel could be safely launched sideways in the hundred-foot-wide dry dock perpendicular to the Maumee River. Zimmer prepared the calculation as best he could, but on launch day a late winter snowstorm producing strong winds forced the river water over the dry-dock gates and up and around the building blocks. As the three thousand spectators anxiously waited in the snow and wind that swirled around them, the flood water, as if teasingly inviting the new vessel to "c'mon in," was already lapping at the ways! This unheard-of situation added such an extra tingle of excitement that the yard super-intendent was seen with a handkerchief in one hand and a

The March 4, 1944, launching of the *Mackinaw* at the American Shipbuilding Yard, Toledo. (Great Lakes Historical Society)

21

A busy *Mackinaw* early in her career.

The *Mackinaw* docked at Cheboygan, Michigan.

An aerial view of the *Mackinaw* showing her helicopter pad.

The stout *Mackinaw* could break solid blue ice five feet thick.

23

tissue in the other. The wife of Vice Adm. Russel R. Waesche scored a perfect hit, smashing the champagne bottle on the bow, but for almost six seconds nothing happened. Finally, she budged and then gracefully slid into the water for a near-perfect launch, while the fear and anxiety of all involved instantly turned into giddy joy. Thus began the career of the *Mackinaw*, born in the snow that would give her life.

With her fitting out and trials completed, the *Mackinaw* was commissioned on December 20, 1944, and placed under the command of her first skipper, Cmdr. Edwin J. Roland. (tour of duty on the *Mackinaw* from December 20, 1944, to January 1, 1946). Although at first Milwaukee was selected as her home port, it was soon changed to Cheboygan, Michigan, so that she would be closer to the heavy traffic in the Straits of Mackinac and the usual menacing ice there. Home port, however, was not where you could find the *Mackinaw* during the first few months of operation. On January 8, 1945, in temperatures hovering around sixteen below zero, she went to work escorting the cargo carriers *Pemiscott, Hildalgo,* and *William L. Nelson* through the St. Marys River after the cutters *Chaparral* and *Sundew* had ushered them down from Whitefish Bay and through the Sabin Lock. It was the first time in history that vessels came through at the Soo Locks and down the St. Marys River in January, and one of the many firsts that the *Mackinaw* accomplished that season. With the navy minesweeper USS *Elusive* nosed snugly into her notched stern, the *Mackinaw* crushed solid ice thirty inches thick and broke twenty-foot windrows from the western end of Lake Erie through the ice-congested lakes to Chicago. The v-notch worked perfectly. It was the first time this sort of operation had taken place and because the vessels were so securely lashed together, men could move back and forth between vessels.

During her first winter of service, while traveling more than fifty-eight hundred miles and making seventeen passages through the Straits, the *Mackinaw* also escorted eight combat vessels from shipyards to their saltwater outlet ports, which, otherwise, would have been icebound until spring. The late Adm. Edwin Roland remembered that he was astonished at the ability of the big cutter to "bust" ice. He recalled how well he liked the bow propeller and how regularly he used it to suck water from beneath the ice to weaken it for easier breaking, while also increasing the flow of water beneath the vessel to "lubricate" the hull and decrease the chances of becoming locked in. Admiral Roland also added

24

The stern of the Big Mac showing the V-notch that was used to tightly secure a vessel, to "become one," and therefore break free from the ice.

The *Mackinaw* with the *S. T. Crapo* locked in its stern V-notch.

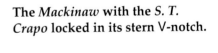

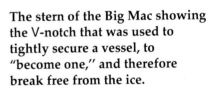

that at one time in northern Lake Michigan he witnessed the *Mackinaw* breaking solid blue ice five to six feet thick. During this busy period, twenty Soviet sailors were taking a six-week training course aboard the *Mackinaw* to learn operational procedures that would later be put to use on several icebreakers that the United States had loaned to the Soviets.

During the spring of 1956, the Canadian government requested U.S. Coast Guard assistance, and the *Mackinaw*, playing Good Samaritan, rendered help to ten vessels locked in the ice of Midland Harbor in lower Georgian Bay. A herculean effort was under way as workers used ice saws to cut four-foot cakes of the solid ice harbor and haul them to the beach in an attempt to free the vessels. The *Mackinaw* worked through the day and all night long breaking solid ice over four feet thick and encountering windrowed ice up to twenty-six feet high. When asked how he knew for sure that the ice was really that thick, Capt. Clifford MacLean said, "Because we hauled a chunk aboard and measured it."

In talking with the present and former skippers and crew members of the *Mackinaw*, each was asked to recollect his most memorable experience aboard. Capt. Gordon Hall, commander of Mac from July 1978 to June 1980, tells about an assist given to the thousand-foot ore carrier *Edwin H. Gott* during her maiden voyage in February 1979, a winter often referred to as the worst one on record. As could be expected, the severest ice encountered during the escort was in the St. Marys River. However, even though they were familiar with the sluggish maneuverability of a thousand-footer in heavy ice, the *Gott* was unusually unmanageable and almost impossible to steer. No wonder, for it wasn't until the *Gott* neared Two Harbors in western Lake Superior that they discovered somewhere behind them they had lost a rudder!

Life aboard Mac for the eight officers and sixty-six enlisted men, though governed by military order and discipline, is nevertheless described as "the best in the service." Facilities for the crew include three lounges, television and recording conveniences, movies (while under way), a small exchange, and a two thousand-volume library said to be the largest of any Coast Guard vessel. Cooks, who receive "excellent" ratings, prepare a wide variety of entrees, which includes prime rib, lobster, and steak; "terrific" desserts and "great" coffee are standard fare.

Working in heavy ice may be thought to be unbearably noisy below for those off watch, but this is not so; at least it is not a cause of aggravation. On the contrary, the hum of the

26

engines and the gentle rolling is enough to rock anyone to sleep.

Bosun Mate Second Class Bill Garrett's most unusual experience is one that few of us will ever have. Imagine standing anchor detail on the bow of the *Mackinaw* as she bumps through the ice in minus forty-degree temperatures during a howling snowstorm. Dressed for the occasion in face mask and goggles Bill says, "It is an exhilarating experience that I not only like but also one that I will never forget."

Capt. F. J. Honke, the skipper of Mac from 1980 to 1983, had many stories about the "unique" vessel, but points to the winter of 1980-81 for a couple of his most remembered predicaments. Fifteen ships were caught in the St. Marys River and the *Mackinaw* spent thirty consecutive days under way, including Christmas and New Year's Day, battling the frozen waterways. His most trying experience was in March 1981 when Mac and three other vessels were caught in seventy-knot-plus winds while "sandwiched" in a vise of treacherous ice that had been swept from the shoreline of Whitefish Bay in Lake Superior. Seized in the massive, wind-driven floe, all four vessels were practically at the mercy of the windblown madness, as they were driven closer and closer to the shore. In a desperate fight to free one of the ships beset in ice, the *Mackinaw* made pass after pass around the vessel. Before a path around the ship was completed, however, the seventy-five-foot swath made by Mac was closed up again with roaring ice. Finally, after four or five hours, the *Mackinaw* won out and was able to work in the floe to decrease the ice pressure enough to set the vessels free, but only when they were dangerously close to the Canadian shore.

The "warm" side of the normally cold Mac story is her participation in the annual Purple Heart Cruise. Irv Kupcinet, a columnist for the Chicago *Sun-Times*, originated the idea that, since 1945, has brought a piece of the "love boat" to many Chicago-area handicapped armed forces veterans. The excursion steamers *North* and *South American* were originally used for the cruise; the *Mackinaw* has acted as the showboat since 1970. Upward of six hundred hospitalized veterans are taken aboard for a six-hour Lake Michigan cruise. But there is a whole lot more in store for the veterans than just cruising off the breakwater in a Coast Guard cutter. The day before the big event, some 125 support and entertainment people come aboard to stock and decorate the ship. Yachting caps, catered box lunches, and refreshments are on hand for everyone.

Lookout Frederick A. McCardell on the bow of the *Mackinaw* on western Lake Michigan December 17, 1983. Temperature 11 degrees; wind chill -33 degrees. (U.S. Coast Guard)

The searchlight on the *Mackinaw* probes the way during a night ice-breaking sortie. (U.S. Coast Guard)

Chicago Bears cheerleaders pose with a vet on one of the *Mackinaw's* Purple Heart cruises. (Courtesy Chicago Sun Times)

Held in mid-July, each cruise takes aboard a cross section of entertainers, who pitch in with one purpose: "to cheer the hearts of our veterans." The Teddy Bears, Chicago Bear cheerleaders, might be on hand to pose for pictures with some of the men. On the forecastle, you might find a famous area disc jockey spinning records while a dance studio is set up to offer lessons in the latest dance steps. There is usually a continual floor show, three different bands, and a handful of comedians. If ever a vessel could be imagined as having its own feelings, it would certainly be the *Mackinaw* bursting with pride during this time. As one veteran commented, it was the only time of the year he got off his hospital grounds.

Often referred to as the "Triple A" of the Great Lakes, the Coast Guard, whose mission has always been to offer assistance in matters of "life or death," continues to extend a helping hand, but is increasingly plagued by the growing number of inexperienced boaters, who, through lack of sea knowledge, find themselves in a perilous situation and call the Coast Guard for help. The executive officer of the *Mackinaw*, Lt. Cmdr. Keith Colwell, states, "The service is free now, but if cutbacks in manpower continue, commercial assistance, instead of Coast Guard help, may become the norm in many cases. What is needed is an even broader program to train boaters before they venture out for the first time."

According to Coast Guard guidelines, the primary duty of the *Mackinaw* is ice breaking, followed by law enforcement, assisting those in distress, cooperating with other government agencies, checking navigational aids, and maintain-

The *Mackinaw* in an early "dawn breaking."

Mac rocks through the "peanut butter" ice in the St. Clair River.

ing military readiness. However, because of the current state of affairs, these priorities may change. During the 1988-89 ice season, operating with an average of eleven cutters, the Coast Guard rendered 193 assists to commercial vessels representing 1,287,489 tons of cargo valued at $195,160,337. They also helped in flood prevention with two missions for a total of 18 1/2 hours. Five hundred eighty-four hours of other miscellaneous assistance was also given.[1] Five hundred man-hours were expended in ice operations and seventy-four hours of air reconnaissance. There were 8,325 search-and-rescue cases reported, 9,014 unit responses, and 13,142 sorties of aircraft and ships. Four hundred fifty-three lives were saved and 124 were lost. In all, 19,350 persons were helped and $10,768,000 worth of private property was saved.

Not long ago, when rumors were flying about the possible decommissioning of the able ship, I took a little survey about what her loss would mean. I talked to ship watchers, ordinary seamen, skippers, and Coast Guard men. Perhaps the sentiment and the need for Mac was best described by one retired lakes captain when I asked what he thought about the decommissioning. He responded almost with a vengeance, "Why, what's gonna bust loose those mountains of ice in the Straits, or in the St. Marys, or the backed-up jam at Algonac? Nothing can put a dent in that 'cept the Mac. Decommission the Mackinaw? They're crazy!"

All that was needed to quiet those who wanted to do away with the *Mackinaw* was an incident like the following. The great "peanut butter" ice jam on the St. Clair River in the early spring of 1984 will long be remembered as one of the most unusual spectacles in the area. Scores of ships were helplessly stuck in a "slush" floe that was believed to be all the way down to the bottom of the river in some areas. Ship watchers in the thousands dotted the shore to view a parade of ships that would not budge. Most of the United States icebreakers and two Canadian breakers were working around the clock to clear the bottleneck, and it was said that they could have used five more Mackinaws! Once again called on to get someone "out of a jam," the *Mackinaw* went to work, in March 1991, six miles from Duluth Harbor, to free the 1,013-foot *Paul R. Tregurtha*, the 1,000-foot *George A. Stinson*, and the 767-foot *Kaye E. Barker*. The vessels were stuck in ice that had packed into the western tip of Lake Superior during the worst freezing-rain storm in twenty-five years. Winds of up to fifty knots created six-foot windrows of ice, which proved too much for the cutter *Sundew* to handle. So, the Mac, once more, was called in to prove her worth. Ship

The Canadian Coast Guard cutter *Griffon*.

The big Canadian cutter *Des Grosseilliers*.

The buoy tender *Acacia*.

The *Katmai Bay* near Marine City, Michigan.

The *Mackinaw* in the St. Marys River in the spring of 1951. For all those who said that "the *Mackinaw* was never stuck."

watchers and fleet owners, however, need not worry for a while. A recent examination of the current condition of the *Mackinaw* determined that she will have, at the minimum, a life extension of five years. There is a good possibility of further extensions after that.

So that is the story of this champion of winter, one of the successors to the great line of pioneer icebreakers. No matter what her work, whether it be her intended purpose, to break ice, or a Good Samaritan, ship watchers will long have a special fondness for the strong and venerable *Mackinaw*.

2. THE *NORONIC*

Though the last mile march ended long ago,
And the sun-filled snapshots have faded,
The memories of "Norey" are so close to me
That they never will be dated.

At the Western Drydock Company yard in Port Arthur, Ontario, on October 24, 1912, a keel was laid for a giant excursion vessel, the largest on the Great Lakes at the time. Born out of the clatter and cacophony of the riveters' hammers, hull number six was designed by the Swedish naval architect Eric Tornoos, who was trying to create the most superb excursion steamer on the inland seas.

Although it might have appeared to the casual observer that not much of anything could possibly be made from the great stacks of material and apparent jumble of supplies cluttering the building site, everything had its place. Each piece of stock was identified and stored according to how it would fit into or onto the ever-growing shape of the 385-foot hull. Steel plates and the boilers were hauled all the way from Cleveland by steamer; the finest birch, ash, pine, and maple for the interior fittings came from forests around Port Arthur.

This new vessel would acquire its name from the merger of the Northern Navigation Company (the owner of the vessel), the Richelieu and Ontario Line, and many smaller companies that would merge June 17, 1913, to form Canada Steamship Lines. The name *Noronic* was given to the vessel in honor of this merger. The letters *no* represented the Northern Navigation Company, the letters *ro* stood for the Richelieu and Ontario Line, and *nic* for the traditional name-ending letters of all the passenger liners of the Northern Navigation Company, which included the *Saronic*, *Hamonic*, and *Huronic*. Later, thousands of romantic honeymooners, dreamy-eyed lovers, raucous high school senior-trippers, and proud crew members would all profoundly claim her as "their Norey."

S.S. NORONIC after launching June 2 1913 Port Arthur Lovelady Photo

The *Noronic* being launched at Port Arthur, Ontario, June 2, 1913. (Courtesy Gene Onchulenko)

The *Noronic* immediately after launching. (Courtesy Gene Onchulenko)

The *Noronic*

Many of the sixty thousand residents of the twin cities of Port Arthur and Fort William (now known as Thunder Bay), Ontario, were planning to attend the launching of the *Noronic*, scheduled for June 2, 1913. The new "boat" was going to be launched although many people, not being familiar with shipbuilding practices, believed that the vessel still appeared incomplete, for only the freshly painted hull was finished. The upper superstructure, including cabins, pilothouse, and stack, was yet to be added. However, when the mayors of the twin cities declared a holiday for the launching, it was proof enough that the new ship was "done" and that something very special was about to take place. To this excitement came the unprecedented announcement that all the area schoolchildren would not only be off half a day, but would be brought to the site in special cars so that they, too, could witness the event.

The light spring rain did not dampen spirits as the final preparations were made ready for the launch. The big steamer *Hamonic* was in town and moored up close to the area so that the hundreds of shipping company officials and businessmen could first be treated to a luncheon aboard and then have the advantage of a perfect view of the spectacle. Little did anyone realize that both of these fine vessels would someday share a horrible fate. But now the shipyard and the surrounding hills were packed full of joyful, excited onlookers anxiously awaiting the first movement of the giant hull. A company director's wife, Mrs. Edward Bristol, broke the champagne bottle across the bow and simultaneously the signal was given to sever the six cables holding the vessel in position. Because the *Noronic* started down the ways so evenly, her first movement was hard to detect. But a deafening roar of the crowd came as the bow and stern met the water at the same time and created a giant wave that drenched and scattered spectators who were trying to edge too close for that special view. At the exact moment the *Noronic* touched the water, every factory, train, and boat whistle in the area was blown to add the final touch and proclaim a perfect launch.

It was fortunate that not until November 29 of that year did the *Noronic* arrive at Sarnia for her final fitting out. The brand-new vessel, which now looked completed but was not, was safe in her berth throughout the worst storms in the history of the Great Lakes, on November 7-11, 1913.

Hundreds of workmen of every skill and trade now converged on the *Noronic* in the final great task of finishing and polishing the splendid vessel. Using the finest materials

The *Noronic* in her fitting-out berth at Port Arthur, Ontario. (Courtesy Gene Onchulenko)

The *Noronic* leaving Port Arthur for Sarnia, Ontario. (Courtesy Gene Onchulenko)

available carpenters swarmed over the vessel, fabricating and installing partitions and panels, custom building tables, stairways, railings, and cabinets, and finishing each gathering room, salon, and stateroom with almost precision workmanship. Exquisite hardwood flooring was then laid down, and highly polished. Next came the painters to lay on countless gallons of varnish, stain, and paint to highlight each room with pleasing effects. Plush carpeting, rugs, drapes, blinds, and curtains were added to offer the right decorative theme without regard to expense. Light fixtures and lamps of every sort were wired in place to add still another facet of beauty to the surroundings. Enough of the most modern kitchen equipment was installed to prepare fine, multicourse meals for the citizens of a small city. Then came an army of suppliers bringing the beds, bunks, wicker chairs, stuffed sofas, blankets, sheets, pillows, pillowcases, towels, napkins,

Early photo of the *Noronic*.
(Great Lakes Historical Society)

tablecloths, glasses, cups, fine dinnerware, silverware, and all the hundreds of necessary odds and ends to efficiently operate a giant floating hotel.

The owners of the *Noronic* did have something special to boast about. The new, spotless, and seemingly flawless vessel had six decks and could carry 562 passengers, and a crew of 187 in 1933. This meant that at capacity there was about one crewman to pamper and serve every three passengers. Her staterooms had beds rather than bunks, which were standard at the time, and most rooms had private baths with running water. The lower-deck rooms, whether an inside or an outside room, had the benefit of the "sea breeze" because of the ingenious layout of large rectangular, vertical windows that ventilated adjoining hallways of each room. The dining salon, situated on a top deck, spanned the entire width of the vessel, could serve 272 people, or almost half of full capacity, at one time, and was surrounded by large "picture" windows, which offered an unobstructed view from every seat. An observation salon, which became a dance hall in the evening, also spread across the entire deck and featured huge upholstered chairs, an elegant inlaid oak floor, and another unimpeded view through large windows. Probably this room would hold the happiest and most vivid memories of anyone who would ride on the *Noronic*. Other special attractions were a social hall, writing room, music room, chapel, smoking room, children's playroom, barber shop, beauty parlor, souvenir concession, lounge, and buffet bar. This assortment of rooms, large and small, offered the passengers a choice of either large gathering areas or quiet retreats during the long cruises. One of the most beautiful design features of the passenger areas was the large, oval well opening in the center of the forward part of A deck, down through the combined observation room and dance hall on B deck, to the social hall on C deck. The edges of these wells were rimmed with magnificent wood banisters and balusters on each deck. Ample air circulation was thus afforded up through the wells, which contained ventilation windows in the ceiling over the dance hall.

Another unusual distinction of the *Noronic* was that she was not only designed as a most luxurious excursion steamer, but also as a freight carrier. This feature allowed her to extend her pre-and post-operating season. She could take your automobile aboard with you for the trip and could carry a deadweight capacity of thirty-two hundred tons, or enough freight to fill $1^{1}/2$ miles of freight cars.

All through the early part and into spring of 1914 the *Noronic* was labored over down to the finest and most complete detail. Even the crow's nest high on the foremast, unusual on a Great Lakes vessel, gleamed brightly with fresh paint. And there she was. The new, pristine lady was lying in her slip ready for a long career. Somehow she surely must have carried a broad smile that day in May 1914 when her short, preseason, maiden voyage took place. Invited dignitaries of every stature and office were aboard to enjoy her elegance and splendor and to revel at the thrill of being "first" to test her every gadget, service, and convenience. Everything worked as it was supposed to, as her crew handled her with such perfection that it seemed as though they had performed their tasks a thousand times before. As this was her first close contact with her future patrons, a careful and sincere regard was paid to safety and security, especially in the light of the recent November storm and the 1912

Sailing Schedule

1937

All times shown are EASTERN STANDARD TIME except where CENTRAL STANDARD TIME is indicated thus (C.T.)

WESTBOUND SAILINGS

Summer Sailings — From Windsor and Detroit. Saturday June 26† and every Monday and Friday thereafter until Sept. 6. Sept. 6 sailing to Port Arthur only.

Spring and Fall Sailings — From Sarnia Saturdays, Thursdays and Tuesdays May 1, 6, 11, 15, 20, 25, 29, June 3, 8, 12, Sept. 11, 16, 21 and 25

		S. S. NORONIC	S. S. HAMONIC		S. S. HAMONIC		
Lv. Windsor, Ont. (Gov't. Dock)	9:30 P.M.	Friday	Monday				
Lv. Detroit, Mich. (Foot Brush St.)	11:00 P.M.	Friday	Monday				
Ar. Sarnia, Ont. (Point Edward)	6:45 A.M.	Saturday	Tuesday				
Lv. Sarnia, Ont. (Point Edward)	4:00 P.M.	Saturday	Tuesday	4:00 P.M.	Saturday	Thursday	Tuesday
Ar. Sault Ste. Marie, Ont. (C.S.L. Dock)	9:45 A.M.	Sunday	Wednesday	9:45 A.M.	Sunday	Friday	Wednesday
Lv. Sault Ste. Marie, Ont. (C.S.L. Dock)	12:00 Noon	Sunday	Wednesday	11:30 A.M.	Sunday	Friday	Wednesday
Ar. Port Arthur, Ont. (Can. Nat. Ry. Dock)①	6:30 A.M.	Monday	Thursday	6:30 A.M.	Monday	Saturday	Thursday
Lv. Port Arthur, Ont. (Can. Nat. Ry. Dock)①	6:30 P.M.	Monday	Thursday				
Ar. Duluth, Minn. (Nor. Pac. Ry. Dock No. 4)	9:00 A.M.	Tuesday	Friday				

† June 26 sailing 9.00 a.m. from Windsor, 9.30 a.m. from Detroit but as shown above at other ports.

EASTBOUND SAILINGS

From Duluth — Every Tuesday and Friday, June 29 to Sept. 7

From Port Arthur — Mondays, Saturdays and Thursdays, May 3, 8, 13, 17, 22, 27, 31, June 5, 10, 14 and Sept. 9, 13, 18, 23, 27

		S. S. NORONIC	S. S. HAMONIC		S. S. HAMONIC		
Lv. Duluth, Minn. (Nor. Pac. Ry. Dock No. 4)	5:30 P.M.	Tuesday	Friday				
Ar. Fort William, Ont.① (C.P.R. Dock)	6:15 A.M.	Wednesday	Saturday				
Ar. Port Arthur, Ont. (Can. Nat. Ry. Dock)①	9:30 A.M.	Wednesday	Saturday				
Lv. Port Arthur, Ont. (Can. Nat. Ry. Dock)①	1:00 P.M.	Wednesday	Saturday	1:00 P.M.	Monday	Saturday	Thursday
Ar. Sault Ste. Marie, Ont. (C.S.L. Dock)	8:30 A.M.	Thursday	Sunday	8:30 A.M.	Tuesday	Sunday	Friday
Lv. Sault Ste. Marie, Ont. (C.S.L. Dock)	10:30 A.M.*	Thursday	Sunday	10:30 A.M.	Tuesday	Sunday	Friday
Ar. Sarnia, Ont. (Point Edward)	6:30 A.M.	Friday	Monday	6:30 A.M.	Wednesday	Monday	Saturday
Lv. Sarnia, Ont. (Point Edward)	Between 10 A.M. and 12 Noon						
Ar. Detroit, Mich. (Foot Brush St.)	4:25 P.M.	Friday	Monday				
Ar. Windsor, Ont. (Gov't. Dock)	5:15 P.M.	Friday	Monday				

①All steamers call at Fort William, Ont. but passengers for or from points in Western Canada are received and discharged only at Port Arthur (3 miles from Fort William)
*Leaves at 12:15 noon Sundays

CONNECTING RAIL SERVICE—WESTBOUND

	FOR SUMMER SAILINGS			FOR SPRING AND FALL SAILINGS			
	FROM TORONTO TO SARNIA						
	Via Canadian National Railway			Via Canadian National Railway			
Lv. Toronto, Ont.	11:30 A.M.	Saturday	Tuesday②	8:30 A.M.	Saturday	Thursday	Tuesday
Ar. Sarnia, Ont.	3:40 P.M.	Saturday	Tuesday	1:10 P.M.	Saturday	Thursday	Tuesday
	(Train runs through to Point Edward Wharf)			(Bus Transfer from Railroad Station to Point Edward Wharf)			

②Does not leave Toronto or arrive Sarnia Sept. 7th.

	FROM PORT ARTHUR TO WINNIPEG				
	Via Can. Nat. Ry.	Via Can. Pac. Ry.	Via Can. Nat. Ry.	Via Can. Pac. Ry.
Lv. Port Arthur, Ont.	6:30 A.M. (C.T.) Mon. and Thur.④	③8:05 A.M. Daily	4:00 P.M. (C.T.) Mondays	③8:05 A.M. Daily
Ar. Winnipeg, Man.	7:50 P.M. (C.T.)	7:45 P.M. (C.T.) Daily	9:10 A.M. (C.T.) Tuesdays	7:45 P.M. (C.T.) Daily

③Connects if steamer arrives on schedule. ④Does not leave Port Arthur or arrive Winnipeg Thursday, Sept. 9th.

CONNECTING RAIL SERVICE—EASTBOUND

	FROM WINNIPEG TO PORT ARTHUR				
	Via Can. Nat. Ry.	Via Can. Pac. Ry.	Via Can. Nat. Ry.	Via Can. Pac. Ry.
Lv. Winnipeg, Man.	10:30 P.M. (C.T.) ⑤ Tues. and Fri.	6:25 P.M. (C.T.) Daily	6:10 P.M. (C.T.) Wed. and Fri.	6:45 P.M. (C.T.) Daily
Ar. Port Arthur, Ont.	11:25 A.M.(C.T.) ⑤ Wed. and Sat.	6:45 A.M. Daily	11:00 A.M. (C.T.) Thurs. and Sat.	7:05 A.M. Daily

⑤Does not leave Winnipeg Tuesday, Sept. 7 or arrive Port Arthur Sept. 8.

	FROM SARNIA TO TORONTO					
	Via Canadian National Railway			Via Canadian National Railway		
	(Train starts at Point Edward Wharf. No Bus Transfer)			(Bus Transfer from Point Edward Wharf to Railroad Station)		
Lv. Sarnia, Ont.	7:40 A.M. Friday	Monday⑥	10:25 A.M. Wednesday	Wednesday	Saturday	Monday
Ar. Toronto, Ont.	11:50 A.M. Friday	Monday	3:40 P.M. Wednesday	Wednesday	Saturday	Monday

⑥Passengers arriving at Sarnia Monday, Sept. 6 transfer by Bus from Point Edward Wharf to Railroad Station for train leaving at 10:25 A.M.

All schedules will be adhered to as closely as possible, but the Company will not hold itself responsible for detention account stress of weather or other unavoidable causes, nor for delayed connections of its own steamers or others, and reserves the right to alter any schedule with or without notice.

Special: Account United States Coasting laws, Detroit passengers going to Duluth or Duluth passengers going to Detroit, must board and leave ships at Windsor, Ont.

Local Passenger Tariff

SPECIAL ROUND TRIP FARES

including passage, meals and berth, good going and returning same steamer or first steamer leaving destination of ticket.

BETWEEN ▼	AND ▼	Inside Berth	Outside Berth	Parlor Room Space
Detroit, Mich. or Windsor, Ont.	Duluth, Minn......	$67.50	$80.00	$109.50
Sarnia, Ont.	Duluth, Minn......	$63.00	$75.50	$97.00

REGULAR PASSAGE FARES—Meals and Berth Additional as shown below

BETWEEN ➤ ▼ AND	•Detroit Windsor		Sarnia		Sault Ste. Marie		Port Arthur	
	One Way	Round Trip	One Way	Round Trip	One Way	Round Trip	One Way	Round Trip
Sarnia, Ont.	$ 1.25	$ 2.50	....	....	....	....	....	....
Sault Ste. Marie, Ont.	12.75	23.50	$11.50	$20.70	....	....	....	....
Port Arthur, Ont.	24.25	43.65	24.25	43.65	$12.75	$23.50	....	....
Duluth, Minn.	•27.75	•50.20	27.75	50.20	16.25	29.50	$6.00	$9.80

MEALS AND BERTH CHARGES PER PERSON

BETWEEN ▼	AND ▼	Inside Berth		Outside Berth		Parlor Room Space	
		One Way	Round Trip ✢	One Way	Round Trip ✢	One Way	Round Trip ✢
Detroit, Mich. or Windsor, Ont.	Sarnia, Ont.	$2.00	$ 4.00	$2.50	$ 5.00	$ 5.00	$10.00
	Sault Ste. Marie, Ont.	6.00	12.00	7.50	15.00	15.00	30.00
	Port Arthur, Ont.	11.00	22.00	12.50	25.00	23.00	46.00
	Duluth, Minn.	•11.50	•23.00	•16.50	•33.00	•30.00	•60.00
Sarnia, Ont.	Sault Ste. Marie, Ont.	5.00	10.00	6.00	12.00	10.00	20.00
	Port Arthur, Ont.	9.00	18.00	10.00	20.00	18.00	36.00
	Duluth, Minn.	11.50	23.00	15.50	31.00	25.00	50.00
Sault Ste. Marie, Ont.	Port Arthur, Ont.	4.50	9.00	5.00	10.00	8.00	16.00
	Duluth, Minn.	8.50	17.00	9.50	19.00	15.00	30.00
Port Arthur, Ont.	Duluth, Minn.	4.00	8.00	4.50	9.00	7.00	14.00

•Passengers between Detroit and Duluth, and vice versa, may be issued tickets good only for continuous round trip on same steamer, as, in accordance with United States coasting laws tickets one way, or round trip season limit, should not be sold reading Detroit to Duluth or vice versa. Passengers desiring such passage should purchase tickets reading between Windsor and Duluth and board and leave steamer accordingly. Convenient taxi service is available going and returning between downtown Detroit and ships' side at Windsor, or Brush Street Dock, Detroit.

✢May be sold only when positive Round Trip reservation has been made.

FARES FOR CHILDREN

(a) A child under five years of age occupying berth with adult or with another child who has paid half adult transportation fare and half charge for meals and berth will be carried free, except when taken to the dining room, a charge will be made for meals as follows:

AND ▼ BETWEEN ➤	Detroit Windsor	Sarnia	Sault Ste. Marie	Port Arthur
Sarnia, Ont.	$0.75	....	....	....
Sault Ste. Marie, Ont.	2.75	$2.00	....	....
Port Arthur, Ont.	4.75	4.00	$2.00	....
Duluth, Minn.	5.75	5.00	3.00	$1.00

	Transportation	Meals and Berth
(b) Child under five years of age occupying berth alone (where such can be provided)	Free	Adult Rate
(c) Two children under five years of age occupying berth together. (See Note "A")	Free	One child at adult rate and one as per paragraph (a)
(d) Child five years of age and under twelve occupying berth alone	Half Rate	Adult Rate
(e) Child five years of age and under twelve sharing berth with another child of similar age	Half Rate	Half Rate
(f) Child five years of age and under twelve sharing berth with an adult or occupying space in room with two adults	Half Rate	Half Adult Inside Berth Rate
(g) Children twelve years of age and over	Adult Rate	Adult Rate

EXCLUSIVE OCCUPANCY OF ROOM

Each room is intended to accommodate at least two adult passengers but one adult may be allowed exclusive occupancy of one whole room on payment of charges as indicated hereunder:

Inside room—One adult passage fare plus two meals and berth charges.

Outside Room or Parlor Room—One and one-half passage fares plus one and one-half adult meals and berth charges as per tariff in effect for class of room occupied.

Note "A"—Irrespective of charges provided in paragraphs (a) and (b) an adult and child or adult and two children may be assigned a whole room only on payment of equivalent of one adult and one-half transportation tickets and two adult meals and berth tickets.

Titanic disaster, which still caused many passengers to be quite wary of shipboard travel.

Everything had progressed without so much as a hint of error. Her launching was called "perfect," she was protected from the killer storm, her fitting-out advanced on a timely, almost carefree, schedule, and her impeccable debut was a smash! How, then, could any one explain the most embarrassing incident that took place while the *Noronic* was loading coal at the Point Edward dock just before her first full season? Having received over four hundred tons of coal into her holds, with the chutes still in place, the big vessel suddenly and severely listed toward the pier, which, fortunately, supported and prevented the potential disaster of capsizing. Mooring lines snapped like thread as water was swallowed down into the open gangways and ports and over the rail of D deck. Luckily, no passengers were aboard nor was anyone around who had recently witnessed her first sailing. Luckily, too, the appalling *Eastland* capsizing at a Chicago dock that would drown 835 souls had not happened yet, for if it had it would be safe to say that this beautiful new vessel would lie idle for lack of passengers.

Without a lot of commotion the situation was brought under control and the great pumps went into action to send the unwanted water overboard to bring the *Noronic* back to a normal level. Workmen then feverishly removed soaked, and yet unused, plush carpeting and rugs and sent them ashore for drying. The affected companionways, stairs, partitions, panels, and floors were cleaned and brought back to par, while inspectors peered through lower superstructure bulkheads for any signs of damage or possible leaks. The *Noronic* came through her first mishap, for the most part, unharmed and would continue the season, but with pig iron added to her number one hold to stabilize and adjust her waterline to a sure-safe level. The incident quickly faded away with the excitement of her first, hitch-free season. However, after her last trip that year, a Lorain dry dock was waiting for the construction of a most unusual addition to her sleek hull "Blisters," or "sponsons," were added to her fifty-two-foot width on each side to offer more stability and increase her beam to 59.6 feet, or almost four feet per side. With this alteration, even though some "lady watchers" would say that it ruined her looks, at least she would not have another rolling or list problem.

So the beautiful lady began a long career of fun-filled, week-long excursions that, during her regular mid-June to mid-September season, originated in Windsor and ran to

Duluth and back. Besides this regular schedule, several special pre-and post-season cruises were usually made; final freight-only trips rounded out the year. In 1933 you could obtain a special round-trip fare for this cruise including passage, meals, and berth in a parlor room (ten available) for $115 per person. Representing the best accommodations on the *Noronic*, the parlor rooms consisted of either twin or double beds, a wardrobe, and a bathroom. For eighty-three dollars, an extra large outside saloon room (34 available) could be acquired. Seventy-five dollars would buy a preferred-location cabin room (92 available) for the cruise, and an inside or an outside corridor room (146 available) was yours

The *Noronic* in the Welland Canal in 1930. (Courtesy Jim Cassin)

45

The Norey on another summer cruise.

The *Noronic* about to pass beneath the Blue Water Bridge, Port Huron, Michigan. (Great Lakes Historical Society)

The *Noronic* always "tooted" when going under the Blue Water Bridge.

The *Noronic* docked beside the *Cayuga*.

for sixty-five dollars. For an additional eighteen dollars, you could take along your automobile.

Warm and affectionate words quickly spread about her elegant surroundings, invigorating activities, and fine cuisine, and soon, thousands of travelers were discovering for themselves the wonderful thrill of her cruises. Oh, you felt like a million dollars when you sailed on the *Noronic*! The ship and the crew seemed to cater to you in particular, so that regardless of any class structure that might have been apparent elsewhere, on the *Noronic* everyone was treated like royalty.

Arriving in Detroit or Windsor from home, you were breathless with anticipation as you boarded about 10:00 P.M. on a Friday. The bellboy (one of sixteen) helped you settle in your room as the vessel made ready for departure. Not too many uninterested guests, no matter how many times they had been aboard before, would miss the thrill of the bon voyage and the night skyline of Detroit as the ship warped away from the dock and headed up the Detroit River and into Lake St. Clair. For those who wanted them, refreshments were served before turning in. Twenty-four-hour room service was available, too. You arrived in Sarnia the next morning about 6:45 and the first big day began after breakfast when buses were standing by to take passengers to the beach picnic at Canatara Park on Lake Huron. This being the first opportunity to get to know your fellow travelers, bathing, dancing, or perhaps golf at the Sarnia Golf Club made "pairing off" easier. Knowing that the ship did not leave until 4:00 P.M., you were eager to take advantage of the long day to seek out and meet new friends. Waiting back at the Point Edward dock with open arms was "your home for the week," the *Noronic*, which may have been unloaded or loaded with tons of freight while you were wiling away the afternoon. She also had taken aboard many more passengers who had just arrived on the 3:30 train from Toronto, the tracks of which ran parallel to the dock.

The whistle gave a long resonant blast announcing that the hubbub and flurry of activity on the dock and the first of the last good-byes were going to begin. This first daytime departure was again an event to behold as those few unlucky ones left behind standing on the dock would wave to you as though you were leaving on an ocean cruise never to be seen again. And wave you did, as well. Whether you had anyone on the dock waving to you or not, you still found yourself saying good-bye with one or two arms. Slipping away from the last shouted good-bye, you were soon beneath the Blue Water Bridge as another blast of the whistle said "hello" to those above. And now, with the first few strains of the Highland piper filtering through the vessel, the mile march was beginning. Absolutely everyone turned out for the march as six times around the ship you went, twice a day, to equal a mile each time. This march was a fun way to help prevent boredom and offer a bit of exercise to pique your appetite. Noticing the thinning out of the crowd after tea, you realized that it was time to freshen up and get dressed for dinner. The appetizing meals were perhaps the one feature that contributed the most to everyone's enjoyment. With the very best food obtainable, and an accent on French and French-Canadian dishes, the painstakingly prepared meals by top chefs, offering generous portions, were served by courteous and attentive waiters and waitresses. Dinnertime gradually slipped into the evening "get together" of community singing or the masquerade party, both of which were popular events for young and old. There was also "horse racing in miniature," a betting race using small horses and jockeys on a track laid out on the ballroom floor. Dancing to the orchestra, the usual windup event of a

Silverware from the Canada Steamship Lines *Noronic.*

A hand towel from the Canada
Steamship Lines *Noronic*.

Saucer from the *Noronic*.

long day, perhaps with a new heartthrob, was definitely the
cause of many shipboard romances. And speaking of
romances, every once in a while, even though the *Noronic*
patron was "always right" and crew conduct and discipline
was kept well in check, a "love boat" type romance still
sometimes flourished.

Miss Helen MacGregor was highly upset. Because of a
reservation mix-up in Montreal, her vacation appeared to be
ruined. Her holiday cruise had been saved for, and looked
forward to, for so long that it seemed her whole life
depended on its planned and happy turnout. She discovered
that instead of having the private room expected, she would
be sharing a room with a complete stranger, another young
lady. This itself was almost too much to bear, but on top of
that, the quarters were near the lounge, where late boisterous laughter and merrymaking, for one who wanted only
peace and quiet, was more than she could take. Half in tears
and half embroiled over the situation, she appeared at the
purser's office with her complaint. Could it have been the
uniform? True, any clean-cut and polished gentleman in a
pressed and spotless uniform no doubt has fluttered many a
young lady's heart. And Ralph Yates, the young purser on
the *Noronic*, took pride in wearing his uniform—so much so,
that you could tell at a glance that much attention and care
was given to his attire. Mr. Yates listened to and then
smoothed out the roughness of Helen's problem, which, now
laid before this handsome official, seemed rather trivial. No
doubt Mr. Yates had the spirit and the congeniality of the
Northern Navigation Company in mind as he swiftly
addressed and rectified the beautiful lady's predicament. . . .
Yet, quite a few cupid arrows were fired from, and into, both
targets. First of all, Miss MacGregor would be the captain's

guest for dinner at the captain's table. Then, from the few vacant rooms left, he secured for Helen the finest stateroom available, no questions asked, and before she could thank him had her luggage transferred to the new quarters.

Now Ralph wished that he was free to see this delightful lady again, but regulations strictly prevented crew members from associating with the passengers. Later that evening, however, Ralph was granted his wish as Miss MacGregor once again appeared at his office with a dilemma. She had lost her room key and needed a replacement. Explaining that there was but one other key that he could use at the time, he first helped her retrace her steps made that evening, looking in chairs, sofas, and hallways for the "lost key." Finally giving up the search, Ralph got the master key, saw Helen to her room, unlocked the door, and with a big "hearts and flowers" sigh said goodnight.

As one of countless romances went, Helen and Ralph

A week of "fun-filled" activities that were available to *Noronic* passengers.

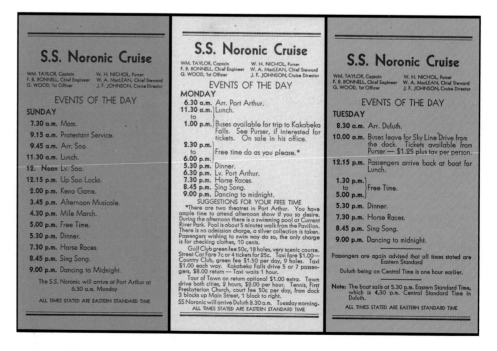

were infatuated with, corresponded with, and saw each other enough to marry three years later and live "happily ever after." The footnote of this romance, however, came at the time of the Yates' first wedding anniversary when Ralph, reflecting on their meeting, courtship, and marriage, stated, "Had it not been for that lost key, we probably would not have ever gotten together," at which time Helen produced the item that she had held close to her heart and had saved for this first anniversary. "You mean this key, Ralph?" she said.

After a cool night's sleep on breezy Lake Huron, your appetite for breakfast was met with mountains of food fit for a king. With a whole day of sailing ahead on Lakes Huron and Superior, the midday climax, the approach to the "Soo," would be one of the most picturesque parts of the whole trip as the ship sailed through the narrow St. Mary's River between the deep green, tree-lined shores. At Sault Ste. Marie you could watch the unbelievable sight of your ship being lifted twenty-one feet in the locks and into Lake Superior.

All night you would sail across a greater part of the deep waters of oceanlike Lake Superior. Afraid to miss even one experience that each moment brought, nearly everyone would be up early for the six o'clock breakfast and be ready for the majestic scenery as the *Noronic* sailed into Thunder Bay. Here rested the "Sleeping Giant," the tiny island that, according to legend, is the body of Hiawatha turned to stone. After the ship docked at Port Arthur, the rest of the

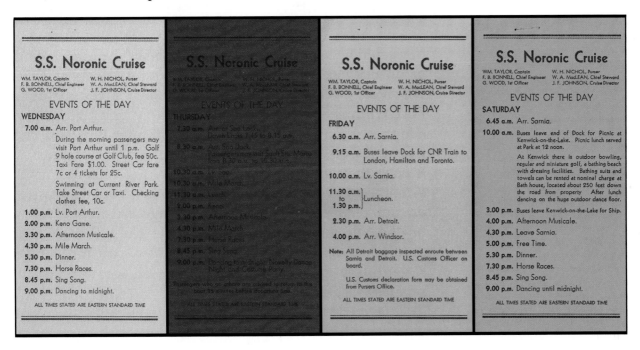

S.S. Noronic Cruise

WM. TAYLOR, Captain   W. H. NICHOL, Purser
F. B. BONNELL, Chief Engineer   W. A. MacLEAN, Chief Steward
G. WOOD, 1st Officer   J. F. JOHNSON, Cruise Director

EVENTS OF THE DAY

WEDNESDAY

7.00 a.m. Arr. Port Arthur.

During the morning passengers may visit Port Arthur until 1 p.m. Golf 9 hole course at Golf Club, fee 50c. Taxi Fare $1.00. Street Car fare 7c or 4 tickets for 25c.

Swimming at Current River Park. Take Street Car or Taxi. Checking clothes fee, 10c.

1.00 p.m. Lv. Port Arthur.

2.00 p.m. Keno Game.

3.30 p.m. Afternoon Musicale.

4.30 p.m. Mile March.

5.30 p.m. Dinner.

7.30 p.m. Horse Races.

8.45 p.m. Sing Song.

9.00 p.m. Dancing to midnight.

ALL TIMES STATED ARE EASTERN STANDARD TIME

S.S. Noronic Cruise

THURSDAY

7.30 a.m. Arr. at Soo Lock.
Down Locks 7.45 to 8.15 a.m.

8.30 a.m. Arr. Soo Dock.
Passengers may visit Sault Ste. Marie from 8.30 a.m. to 10.30 a.m.

10.30 a.m. Lv. Soo.

10.30 a.m. Mile March.

11.30 a.m. Lunch.

2.00 p.m. Keno.

3.30 p.m. Afternoon Musicale.

4.30 p.m. Mile March.

7.30 p.m. Horse Races.

8.45 p.m. Sing Song.

9.00 p.m. Dancing to midnight. Novelty Dance Night and Costume Party.

Passengers who go ashore are advised to return to the boat 15 minutes before departing time.

ALL TIMES STATED ARE EASTERN STANDARD TIME

S.S. Noronic Cruise

WM. TAYLOR, Captain   W. H. NICHOL, Purser
F. B. BONNELL, Chief Engineer   W. A. MacLEAN, Chief Steward
G. WOOD, 1st Officer   J. F. JOHNSON, Cruise Director

EVENTS OF THE DAY

FRIDAY

6.30 a.m. Arr. Sarnia.

9.15 a.m. Buses leave Dock for CNR Train to London, Hamilton and Toronto.

10.00 a.m. Lv. Sarnia.

11.30 a.m.
   to   }Luncheon.
1.30 p.m.

2.30 p.m. Arr. Detroit.

4.00 p.m. Arr. Windsor.

Note: All Detroit baggage inspected enroute between Sarnia and Detroit. U.S. Customs Officer on board.

U.S. Customs declaration form may be obtained from Pursers Office.

ALL TIMES STATED ARE EASTERN STANDARD TIME

S.S. Noronic Cruise

WM. TAYLOR, Captain   W. H. NICHOL, Purser
F. B. BONNELL, Chief Engineer   W. A. MacLEAN, Chief Steward
G. WOOD, 1st Officer   J. F. JOHNSON, Cruise Director

EVENTS OF THE DAY

SATURDAY

6.45 a.m. Arr. Sarnia.

10.00 a.m. Buses leave end of Dock for Picnic at Kenwick-on-the-Lake. Picnic lunch served at Park at 12 noon.

At Kenwick there is outdoor bowling, regular and miniature golf, a bathing beach with dressing facilities. Bathing suits and towels can be rented at nominal charge at Bath house, located about 250 feet down the road from property. After lunch dancing on the huge outdoor dance floor.

3.00 p.m. Buses leave Kenwick-on-the-Lake for Ship.

4.00 p.m. Afternoon Musicale.

4.30 p.m. Leave Sarnia.

5.00 p.m. Free Time.

5.30 p.m. Dinner.

7.30 p.m. Horse Races.

8.45 p.m. Sing Song.

9.00 p.m. Dancing until midnight.

ALL TIMES STATED ARE EASTERN STANDARD TIME

That "special" *Noronic* stateroom key.

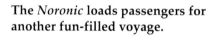

The *Noronic* loads passengers for another fun-filled voyage.

day could be used for shopping, sightseeing, bathing, hiking, or picnicking. You could explore beautiful Kakabeka Falls, which lay twenty-three miles west, take a streetcar ride to Fort William, make a day of swimming or picnicking at Chippawa Park, go golfing at the Thunder Bay Golf and Country Club, or just take a long hike. One-way passengers, leaving the ship here, could make easy train connections to Winnipeg and points west. Regardless of what you chose to do, you enjoyed the most popular fringe benefit of cruising on the *Noronic*, the extended layover time. By 6:30 that evening all were back aboard, ready to depart for Duluth, ravenously hungry for dinner, which was already in progress.

Imagine the sight of the *Noronic* with every porthole and window ablaze with light, skimming along on her last leg en route to Duluth. What a spectacular sight she must have been. I am sure that if you could have somehow been out there in that westbound Lake Superior channel aboard another vessel, so that she could pass you close by, the sight of her speeding along at eighteen miles per hour, all aglow, would have taken your breath away. Some said that because of the addition of her sponsons, her speed was diminished. But not having any accurate means of checking speed unless compared with another vessel, say, running alongside it during a race, her passengers were well satisfied that if she was not the fastest excursion vessel going, certainly she was one of the fastest. Conjecture by anyone who doubted her speed was, nevertheless, put to rest when she would easily "whip" opponents such as the *Keewatin* during many of the "unofficial" races said to have taken place.

As soon as the sun set in all the grandeur possible on the wide horizon of orange splendor that the *Noronic* was racing into, it became noticeably chilly, so that stepping out on deck after the evening's "warm" activities made you think that it was a midwinter night. Cool and crisp, the air on a moonlit Lake Superior night was therapy aplenty to soothe whatever ailment you had.

A wedding portrait of Mr. and Mrs. Ralph Yates.

Before breakfast the *Noronic* would glide under the famous Aerial Bridge, and if you happened to miss that sight, the bustle of one of the largest grain ports in the world told you that you were in Duluth. Because many of the points of interest were within easy walking distance of the dock, it would be convenient to have lunch aboard the *Noronic* for it was included in your fare. Departing Duluth at 4:30 P.M., the ship would proceed out into Lake Superior once again to begin her long journey back, retracing her route. You would arrive dockside in Detroit at 3:30 on a Friday afternoon, most of the time, as advertised, "feeling like a different person."

On July 17, 1945, her sister, the *Hamonic*, was destroyed by fire at a Point Edward dock. On September 17, 1949, during a special postseason Thousand Island's cruise, the thirty-six-year career of the *Noronic* ended. She docked in Toronto that Friday about six in the evening, her bow to the north and starboard side alongside the Canada Steamship Lines pier number nine at the foot of Yonge Street. Like so many times before, she carried 524 carefree passengers and a crew of 171 on what was to have been another happy cruise. Instead, while many of her guests and crew were still enjoying the late evening in the city, a fire that originated in a small linen closet just forward of the women's washroom

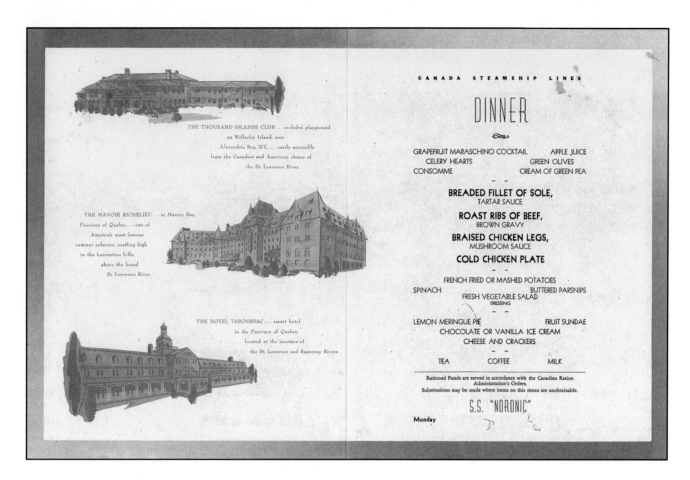

A Monday dinner menu from the *Noronic*.

opening onto the port corridor of C deck took hold and quickly spread due to twelve-mile-per-hour southwest winds. The actual cause of the fire, discovered about 1:30 A.M. by a passenger, Mr. Church, was never established, although two passengers, earlier on this same cruise, observed maids smoking cigarettes in the linen closet, which often contained a large cardboard carton for wastepaper and other refuse. Church saw what he thought was a haze near the aft part of the starboard corridor on C deck as he entered the area from the lounge at the stern. The haze, which turned out to be smoke, was coming from around the locked door of the linen closet. Hearing the sound of fire in the closet and thinking someone was inside, he knocked heavily on the door and then ran forward to the social hall, shouting that the ship was on fire. Meeting the head bellboy, O'Neil, amidships, Church told him of the fire and they both returned to the closet.

At this point there is confusion whether or not O'Neil had the key for the closet on his person or if he had to run back amidships and down the main stairs to the steward's office for the key. Precious, fatal seconds were fast ticking away—seconds that possibly could have been used to prevent the disaster. At any rate, after O'Neil unlocked the door he discovered that the fire extinguisher he had taken from the rear of the ship was not enough to quench the fire, which already had spread into the corridor. Both Church and O'Neil went aft in the port corridor to get the hose from a fire hydrant there. Frantically running the hose forward to the closet, although the valve was said to have been open, no water came from the hose. By this time flames were engulfing the ceiling of the corridor and spreading both directions as far as one could see. Church now noticed that the intense heat from the blaze was volatilizing the paint and varnish of the corridor and was horrified to see how quickly the flames spread. Knowing that the situation was hopeless, he ran down to D deck, woke his family, and left the ship. It is estimated that five minutes went by from the time that O'Neil met Church (to learn of the fire) to when O'Neil turned in the fire alarm. The first equipment of the Toronto Fire Department arrived at the scene about 1:41 A.M. to find the ship almost totally in flames except for parts of the bow and stern.

A fire in the middle of the night aboard a heavily occupied excursion vessel certainly was a highly dreaded misfortune. However, this was no ordinary fire. The raging firestorm that swept through the *Noronic* that night was so fierce, so glowing, and so quickly overpowering that it appeared to have the grim characteristics of an oxygen or a gasoline fire. The reason for this holocaust was that the fire, starting at the port quarter, was not only fanned by the wind from the southwest, but was further sucked up through corridors and hallways to the well openings in A, B, and C decks and out through the open ventilation windows at the top of the dance floor. Thus, the violent, white-hot fire spread quickly beyond containment and raced through the interior of the ship, which acted as a giant flue, intensifying the blaze like a blacksmith's forge.

Finally, the whistle moaned for the last time in a futile attempt to warn those aboard of the obvious disaster. In the ensuing panic, those who failed to escape from the thick smoke perished along with others who were too afraid to jump from the high decks into the dark water below. Many others, who never responded to the late alarm, slept away, succumbing to smoke inhalation. In all, 118 passengers died. Although there were but 15 of the 171 crew members aboard at the time, none of the crew was lost.

Even though there was an ample amount of land-based fire-fighting equipment there, it was almost useless, for

Fire envelops the *Noronic* at Toronto in 1949. (Dossin Great Lakes Museum)

Firemen pour water through her side windows. (Dossin Great Lakes Museum)

The *Noronic* still smolders the morning after the fire. (Dossin Great Lakes Museum)

water that was sprayed into the intense flames immediately turned to steam and did nothing to stop the fire. Ironically, so much water was sent aboard that the charred and forlorn lady sank on the spot, a total loss. Ralph Yates, blinded with tears, boarded the burnt out vessel three days later and cut a section of the steering pole off, with the singed flag still attached, to protect and preserve one of the few unblemished parts of the ship.

According to the Court of Investigation's report about the disaster, the causes for the loss of the Noronic and for the loss of life aboard were due to failure by the owners and the master to: (1) have a patrol of the ship to detect a fire; (2) have any organization operative when the ship was in dock by which information as to the outbreak of a fire could be dispatched to those who could fight a fire; (3) contemplate the possibility of a fire occurring at a dock; (4) have a plan for arousing and getting passengers off the ship in the event of a fire; and (5) train the crew to take proper steps on discovery of a fire or in fire-fighting methods.

Not until three years later were all the litigation and damage claims finally settled for $2,150,000.

The following account of the fire, as seen from the standpoint of the crew members, was related by the former assistant purser, Atholl Murray, who was on the *Noronic* at the time of the fire.

These are some of the details of the *Noronic* fire as we from the crew saw them. Please keep in mind that this was considered an international incident and as far as we were concerned the official inquiry and the facts were, to a certain extent, two different stories.

We have always believed that the fire was the result of a deliberate act of arson, not of a maid's cigarette butt.

The fire broke out on deck just ahead of the stack, on the port side. Because of the direction of the wind, it cut the ship in two. The first and third officers were on duty on the bridge, the crew were in their quarters at the stern.

The mates tried to blow the fire alarm on the klaxon horn, one long, two short, one long. However, the horn "jammed" and blew a continuous blast. This was the signal to abandon ship which the crew did—going over the stern.

It is interesting to note that the klaxon horn was saved from the *Hamonic*, which burned in 1945.

You have to realize that a ship is most vulnerable when it is at dock. This is so because she is listing toward the dock for loading. Therefore, one half of her lifeboats cannot be used because of the dock, the other half cannot be used because of the list. On top of this, your fire hoses are at less than half pressure because the ship's engines are at rest.

As far as I personally am concerned, there was only one person who died inside the ship, and that was because of a heart attack.

The deaths all occurred on the hurricane deck. You see, it is the natural instinct of people caught in a fire to get *above* the fire. This is the worst thing to do because this is where the fire is the hottest. We even pulled one man out of the crow's nest.

When the fire broke out, the boat deck was full of people taking a late night walk or just enjoying the view of the skyline or enjoying the warm night before turning in. The fire ran down this deck and instead of going into the ship and moving to the gangways they (passengers) panicked. They climbed up to the hurricane deck and got trapped. The hurricane deck was the only wooden deck on the ship and consequently was burned out from underneath them. As this deck was actually the roof over the well opening, when it burned through, the bodies of victims, who had already perished from the fire, fell through to various decks below and therefore were found inside the ship.

The following errors were made on the part of the fire department: (1) they would not let the crew back on the ship to fight the fire; (2) they would not let the tugs pull the ship out into the harbor so that we could be out of the wind, which was blowing the fire onto the ship; (3) you cannot fight a ship's fire from the outside; it has to be fought from the inside. The firemen were quite content to pour water onto the ship from the dock—and they would not allow the crew, nor would they go on board themselves, to fight the fire.

It is interesting to note that only three decks of the ship were burned. If you went aboard her after she had been refloated, you would have seen that anything below C deck was not even scorched. The tragedy was the result of a series of errors. A ship is not a building. Therefore you cannot fight a ship's fire as you would a fire on shore. The crew were highly trained and they followed the klaxon's warning. They did not, under any circumstances, panic or desert. They did what they were trained to do. It was true that the captain was ashore. However, the mates were on duty and at their posts. After all, even a captain was allowed shore leave. He was suspended at full pay and the following spring was given the newest flagship of the fleet. These are the impressions of the fire as I experienced them. I believe anyone of the crew would concur. The tragedy of this whole catastrophe can be attributed to panic, the nature of the wind, the ignorance of the fire department, and quite frankly, the search for a scapegoat. The *Noronic* was a fine ship, her crew were excellent, and she had a captain who was the best master that ever sailed the lakes. He died of a broken heart over this catastrophe and was as much a victim as those poor souls who died in the fire.

Longtime *Noronic* excursionist, Paul Hurt, from St. Clair, Michigan, visited me during my work on the *Noronic* painting. When he first saw the canvas, the happy light in his eyes was not enough to conceal the lump in his throat. He and his wife, Mary Frances, had spent their honeymoon on the Norey in 1941, and the memory of "those days" hit him happily but hard. At the time, I had yet to paint in at least three hundred tiny, half-inch passengers on the decks of the *Noronic* as she was portrayed just pulling away from the

A portion of the *Noronic*'s steering pole with singed flag.

59

Honeymooners Mr. and Mrs. Paul Hurt on one of their many trips aboard the *Noronic*. (Courtesy Paul Hurt)

dock at Point Edward on one of those happy excursions. Being honored to know that my work could bring this reaction, I invited Paul and his wife to board the *Noronic* "one more time." He didn't follow my thinking. I explained that because I had all those people to paint in, if he would bring me a snapshot of him and his wife, I would "paint them in" for a final cruise. Paul had a whole album of photos and was thrilled to be in the painting with his bride. The idea caught on and through eventual newspaper articles and radio interviews in many old *Noronic* port cities, some seventy-eight photographs poured in from other past excursionists, honeymooners, and high school seniors. For sure, the "Norey" lives!

3. THE *STEWART CORT*

First of the giants, built super-strong.
Can you imagine, a thousand feet long?
Old-timers scoffed, said she'd break in two.
But on she sails, like she's still brand-new.

Each year they made them bigger. From the early days of shipbuilding on the Great Lakes, each time a new vessel slid down the ways, by some standard or dimension, it was bigger than its predecessor. And by the way a fleet owner or a ship's crew would boast that "their lady" was the largest on the lakes, sometimes by just a few feet more than an earlier bottom, it would seem that the only reason bigger and bigger ships were built was because of foolish rivalry, when, of course, it was due to the pressing demand for more and more cargo space.

Some ship watchers refuse to look at them. It is almost as if these new giants are an abomination that represents a slap to their knowledge of how a ship should look, based on their reminiscences of older vessels. True, compared to the romantic sailing era of Great Lakes vessels, the "super ships," save their majesty of sheer size, are hard to envision as beautiful. Still, I believe any vessel viewed in her element in the right circumstance has a mystic, even charming, beauty.

The drive to build a larger vessel reached a milestone when the *David Dows*, a five-masted brigantine, was built in Toledo in 1881. This spectacular pioneer bulk carrier, the first five-masted vessel in the world, had eight hatches, a wood hull strapped with iron, and eighteen sails made up of 18,630 square feet of canvas. She was designed to carry ninety thousand bushels of grain or three thousand tons of coal, but she never carried a full cargo because of the shallow water in many ports at the time. Although it seemed that shipbuilders' dreams were racing too far ahead of practical and efficient design, progress did not stand idle.

The *David Dows*, built near the end of the sailing era, had a rather short life, but nonetheless offered those endowed with the grandiose dreams of shipbuilding a hint of what

The 1,004' *Edgar B. Speer* caked with ice. (Courtesy Tim Slattery)

was on the horizon. As the maritime community and ship watchers alike marveled at the size of this early giant, it must have been conjectured that no future hull design could possibly surpass such an enormous and strongly built vessel. But the spirited imagination and ingenuity of Great Lakes naval architects and shipbuilders would be restrained only by the limits of their dreams.

Another early leader in the grand procession of firsts was born with the launching of the 280-foot *Onoko* in 1882. The first to be built of iron, this vessel would become the proto-type granddaddy of that distinctive long and narrow vessel unique to the inland seas.

Beauty or beast, *Hull Number 101*, the first supergiant of the lakes, was so profoundly unique that her unusualness, some say, made up for her ugliness. She bounded so far ahead of her nearest counterpart that lakemen today still marvel at her strength and construction. Her hull configuration would be a one-of-a-kind design built especially for only one loading and discharge port. More than merely another of the largest in the annals of lakes shipbuilding, this vessel would be one of the last of the old cabins-forward, tra-ditional freighter designs and would still hold the distinction of being the first thousand-footer on the Great Lakes.

The keels for her bow and stern sections were laid in February 1969 in Pascagoula, Mississippi. These two units were welded together, and "shipped" to the Litton Industries yard at Erie, Pennsylvania, for separation and joining to the seventeen 48' x 105' modules under construc-tion there. Contrary to conventional construction, this most unusual concept of module shipbuilding caused strange morsels of information to flow from the shipyard around Erie. How could a ship of this magnitude be built in this

The *Stewart J. Cort*

manner? Old skippers were already skeptical of a thousand-foot vessel, but to build the thing like a prefab house was doubly questionable. It seemed, however, that her designers were ready to dispel any such fear, for this vessel was to be built *extra* strong to guard against any weakness in her added length. This soon-to-be giant would have 1^{1}/4" steel plates and unusually small hatch openings of 18' x 40'. This would greatly bolster her strength and make her, some said, "as strong as a battleship." A 72-foot bow section complete with bridge and air-conditioned crew accommodations was joined to a 110-foot stern section (with power plant) to form the 182-foot vessel that became known as "Stubby." The width of this runty looking ship could be no wider than 72 feet so that she could squeeze through the Welland Canal. So, the outboard extensions of her bow and stern, the sections that would make up her finished 105-foot beam, were carried aboard, rather than built into the mini-ship. In March 1971 "Stubby" sailed the twenty-six hundred-mile trip through the Gulf of Mexico, up the Atlantic coast, and down the St. Lawrence to Erie. Even more hilarious than the strange look of this powerful, yet miniature, ship were the "Cut here" instructions for the Erie yard workers painted neatly on her sides.

Maybe this was the reason there was doubt of her strength. Cut a ship in half? No one ever heard of it. When it was realized that they were going to take a vessel and cut through it like butter, some questions may have been raised about her stoutness, for usually one thinks there is more to a vessel, internally, than just the skin.

When the seventeen modules were welded together and complete, this 815-foot midbody was made ready to accept "Stubby," which was "cut along the dotted line." First, the bow section was welded in place, then the vessel was towed from the flooded dry dock and positioned to accept the stern section. Now finally a complete hull, the first thousand-footer was moved into a nearby slip for the completion of her outfitting.

This new vessel would be named the *Stewart J. Cort*, after a former vice president and director of Bethlehem Steel who died in 1958. The largest vessel operating then was only 730 feet, so adding 300 feet in one piece of shipbuilding was something to talk about. Her length brought about many comparisons. You could put three football fields end to end and have 50 feet left over. A super fly ball hit 450 feet could be caught about midway on her deck. The USS *Enterprise* (CVN-65) carrier is 100 feet longer, the *Titanic* was 118 feet

The joined stern and bow sections of "Stubby" Hull #1173.
(Great Lakes Historical Society)

shorter, and if you laid two Washington Monuments down end to end, they would be only 110 feet longer than this new monster. In shipping circles, other talk told of her massiveness in yet another direction. During these times, year-round navigation on the lakes was something still in the offing. But the *Cort*, it was thought, could plunge through a solid Lake Michigan, be her own icebreaker, and be the first vessel to run in this manner for an entire winter.

Her fitting out was completed and with little fanfare Mrs. Stewart J. Cort christened the big vessel in the water at Erie, May 4, 1971. In July she sailed out of Erie for the first time for her trials, which would take place out of the shipping lanes in Lake Erie west of Long Point. Her exercises included: (1) a full-speed run of 16½ miles per hour (later to reach 15 miles per hour loaded) to a crash stop in about thirty-two hundred feet and 5½ minutes, far less than other smaller ships; (2) a 360-degree turn within 1,605 feet; (3) letting go and retrieving her three anchors; (4) lowering her single rescue boat and six self-launching life rafts; and (5) testing the smooth performance of her bow and stern thrusters against various beam-wind velocities. All these operations went very well as the new vessel handled superbly and with acute responsiveness. Only one problem was evident but it was one that would present many headaches and delays. The problem was caused by an unusual electrical field created by the turning of a large wheel in her self-unloading system. This mysterious field, in turn, would set up a static charge that interrupted and ill advised a computer to command over a hundred cargo doors when to open and close, much like the shutter of a camera. If this error could not be rectified, it me ant that some of these doors would open, spilling tons of cargo out at the wrong times, while other doors would remain stubbornly closed.

Her technical problems solved, her maiden voyage was planned for the spring opening of the shipping season in April 1972. But Mother Nature had her own planned setbacks. The first trip was delayed a week by serious ice conditions on the lakes. Finally, on May 1, after an all-night anchorage near Erie Light because of fog, the big *Cort* raised anchor and headed upbound for Taconite Harbor, Minnesota, where she would pick up her first cargo of iron ore pellets bound for Burns Harbor, Indiana.

Veteran ship watchers would be the first to know, for sure, of her coming, but the news spread fast and soon thousands of curious spectators were lining the shores en route to

66

The *Cort* shows off her 105-foot beam in this photo taken from the Blue Water Bridge. (Dossin Great Lakes Museum)

catch a glimpse of this first "real" giant. The new ship and its proud master, Capt. Edward P. Fitch, would offer and answer many salutes and greetings along the way. It was a charming custom to salute those on shore, but in this case it was a "hello" of profound distinction because of the *Cort's* unusual whistle. (The term whistle is a misnomer carried over from the sailing days when those vessels carried a shrill-sounding whistle. More aptly, the whistles on today's vessels should be called horns.) She would really have two *horns*, one at her bow and one on her afterdeck house, which, when blown, offered a strange two-toned sound, delayed a split second between tones.

Schoolchildren along her route were let off school so that they could note the passing of this big piece of history. Businessmen, fishermen, and a wide throng of laborers from every workplace took off, or were let off, to see the spectacle. One person went a step further in requesting a special salute when the *Cort* passed. The son of eighty-four-year-old ship watcher Eli "Peck" LeBlanc asked the *Detroit News* if the *Cort* would salute his father in Morse code as she passed. Being that the *Cort* was so modern, she did not even carry a signal lamp, but Bethlehem Steel Corporation went to the trouble to find and have flown to the ship a strong, hand-held spot lamp that would do the job. The *Cort* signaled "Hi Peck" while passing the requested area and even added "73" (the old-time telegraphers signal for "best wishes") but the signals were not understood. Mr. Peck, a former railroad telegrapher, was familiar with a key telegraph, not the newer "blinker" signals that came from the Cort. Even so, the kind gesture was warmly appreciated and is a good example of the fond relationship that exists between a vessel's crew and the ship watchers on shore.

The forty-two-year-old Detroit fireboat, *John Kendall*, spouted a vast water geyser of congratulations as the *Cort* passed Detroit. She was further welcomed by a vast escort of pleasure craft of all types and sizes. A similar flotilla followed her practically all the way through the Detroit River, Lake St. Clair, and the St. Clair River, coaxing as many salutes out of the "big girl" as they could. Thousands of people had filled every riverside park and vantage point along the St. Clair River, including the rails of both the Ambassador and Blue Water bridges. At Marine City, Michigan, the *Cort's* loudspeaker bellowed "You're my kind of people" to the excited crowd waving and pleading for "just one more" response. At Port Huron someone with "*Cort* fever" set off a small display of fireworks and the *Cort* responded with a quick salute. About 7:47 P.M., May 3, the *Cort* passed beneath the Blue Water Bridge to begin her long trip up the lakes.

Everything about the *Cort* was big. This thousand-foot behemoth displaced 67,800 tons and, under normal circumstances, had about 150,462 square feet of wetted surface. Her four General Electric diesels offered fourteen thousand shaft horsepower to her two, controllable pitch, eighteen-foot-diameter propellers. Her electrohydraulic steering gear incorporated dual power units that could move her two massive rudders hard over from forty-five degrees on one side of the ship to forty degrees on the other side in twenty-five seconds. A six-foot diameter tunnel runs completely through the lower structure of the hull at the bow and the stern, which house the thrusters. Four 750-horsepower DC

drive motors turn the thruster propellers to push the ship back and forth in tight areas. This equipment, in essence doing the work of several harbor tugs, can assist nicely in berthing the big lady.

It has been stated that a vessel like the *Cort* could carry 647 tons of cargo one mile on a gallon of diesel fuel. During average trips in good weather, the *Cort* gulps eighty thousand gallons of fuel a week! Her unloading equipment alone would stagger one not used to seeing such enormous amounts of material and mechanical bulk. One of the conveyor belts, a 1 1/4" x 10', steel-cable core, rubber monster, revolves around the sixty-foot unloading wheel. This wheel, driven by the belt, carries the ore pellets in much the same principle as a water-mill wheel. Other belts travel the length of the ship and help with the chore of discharging taconite pellets. (I often wondered, while peering at these gigantic pieces of rubber deep in the bowels of a ship, what would happen if one of them broke—how could they ever replace it?) For the record, the *Cort* could discharge up to twenty thousand tons per hour; however, because the shore equipment normally cannot take her cargo as fast as she can discharge it, her usual discharge rate is about seven thousand tons per hour. This unloading apparatus, a virtual design miracle, would enable her to establish a record turnaround time from "tie up" to "let go" in two hours and fifty minutes, discharging about fifty-six thousand tons of pellets. This shortened turnaround time would probably be the only complaint of the crew, for they are reluctant to go "up the street" (Great Lakes sailors' term for liberty) for fear of missing the expedited sailing of the ship.

The *Cort* displaces 67,800 tons and usually has about 150,462 square feet of wetted surface. (Great Lakes Historical Society)

69

A former skipper of the *Cort*, Capt. Bob Brabander, had not a single dislike of the ship he mastered for seven years. Small wonder The accommodations, duty, chow, and nearly everything that makes life better aboard a Great Lakes freighter during the long season was all part of the "first class" realm of the *Cort* according to present and former crew members. Consisting usually of twenty-nine men, her crew enjoyed mostly private, 16' x 20' rooms, each complete with television, shower, and head. Everyone lives forward in an atmosphere of quiet, far away from the noise and vibration associated with the stern quarters on other vessels. In particular, a deckhand who might earn about twenty-five hundred dollars a month likes the hydraulically operated and secured hatch covers, which can be manipulated by one man. In general, one of the most liked and talked about attributes of the *Cort* was the secure feeling crew members had knowing their vessel was built stronger, perhaps several times stronger, than previous Great Lakes vessels.

Because it is the *first* thousand-foot vessel, a series of wave height and springing research experiments was performed aboard the *Cort* during 1978-81. Forty-two sensors, installed on each side of her bow and over her prow, fed

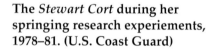

The *Stewart Cort* during her springing research experiements, 1978–81. (U.S. Coast Guard)

A Coast Guard helicopter drops equipment to the deck of the *Stewart Cort* for wave-height experiments. (U.S. Coast Guard)

data into computers to test the ability of the giant to withstand sea conditions over her length. The wavering motion, which moved down her deck in heavy seas, was said to have been much less than in other vessels. She was a guinea pig for six years, and the tests favored her superior strength and dispelled many of the fears of those who believed she was just too big.

The largest vessel now on the lakes is the 1,013-foot *Paul R. Tregurtha*. This could be the last giant from a Great Lakes shipyard for some years to come. Shipbuilding, not just on the Great Lakes, but worldwide, has come to a virtual standstill from overbuilding amid drastic declines in cargo.

The first thousand-footer at work.
(Photo Art of America)

4. THE *SEEANDBEE*

She was a great liner in her day.
Her travels were smooth and far.
And though it was hard to make her pay,
She proved her glory by winning a war.

When famed naval architect Frank E. Kirby signed his name to the work drawings of hull number 190, he penned a master stroke. Like his other famous creations, the steamers *Tashmoo* and *Greyhound*, Detroit & Cleveland Navigation liners, and many other luxurious vessels, this design work, too, without a doubt, would produce another masterpiece. This vessel, however, acclaimed as the absolute crescendo of all his works, would have a dual career and become distinctly renowned in her later one. I wonder what Kirby would have thought if he'd known that this vessel would someday become a crucial element in deciding the outcome of a great world war.

In 1892, even though great opportunities existed for lower Lake Erie passenger trade, the Detroit & Cleveland Navigation Company declined a proposal to extend their service between Cleveland and Buffalo. Instead, under agreement, a syndicate was formed allowing the D&C steamers *City of Alpena*[2] and *City of Mackinac*[3] to be used in this new venture of one year. From this syndicate came the Cleveland and Buffalo Transit Company, which began operation in 1893. The young company read well the need for passenger service. By 1896, to bolster passenger and freight capacity, the new steamer *City of Buffalo*[4] replaced the steamer *State of New York*. In addition, they added the 320-foot *City of Erie* in 1898. The company grew and prospered and by 1911 a bulging 400 percent increase in earnings since their first year of operation, along with a bright forecast for additional capacity on the horizon, directed them to let the contract for hull number 190 to the Detroit Ship Building Company of Wyandotte, Michigan, on April 25, 1912.

Obviously, a supersized excursion steamer was required to fulfill the need.

Now with the horror accounts of the terrible April 15, 1912, *Titanic* disaster still fresh and lingering in most newspapers, one might imagine the obstacles the Cleveland & Buffalo Transit Company faced. The security, strength, and most important, the safety of this unborn vessel had to be instilled in the minds of their future customers. Perhaps that is why it was said that this new vessel was the most advertised ship in the world. The 50-foot long by 98.6-foot beam giant was to be the largest and most costly excursion vessel on the Great Lakes. Naval architects were asserting that this vessel carried the maximum efficiency of this class of steamer to its utmost reaches and that there was nothing beyond. Kirby, himself, reportedly said that he would never design a larger side-wheeler. Employing the *look* of the times, she would be the only Great Lakes vessel to carry four smokestacks. Used as a symbol of strength and majesty on the *Titanic, Olympic, Mauritania,* and other great ocean liners, the use of four stacks offered an aura of security and stability.

Thus, the ship's design and many of the systems were created with an extra cautious eye toward safety. The vessel would have a steel hull divided into three great compartments by fireproof doors extending from the main deck to the dome. Steel fire curtains would be fitted in cargo spaces opposite engine room enclosures. The beams and undersides of the promenade deck would be sheathed with galvanized iron and heavy asbestos paper. This safeguard, coupled with the steel housings up to this deck, would make the vessel, it was said, practically fireproof. She would have a double bottom, divided both longitudinally and transversely into fourteen water tight compartments. Above the water bottom, the hull would be further divided by eleven transverse watertight bulkheads extending from the keel to the main deck. Two trimming tanks, each with a capacity of fifty-two tons on either side of the ship, could be filled or emptied in two minutes, allowing for the vessel to maintain an even keel. Most assuredly, this addition was to dispel any fears of the vessel capsizing.

Besides the sectors already mentioned, the great ship would be also divided into fifty sections for fire alarm purposes, each space containing about eight staterooms along with an ingenious device by which any disturbance would be announced in the engine room and the captain's quarters. The vessel would have a sprinkler system throughout the

The *Seeandbee*

ship. Fire hydrants were to be located throughout the ship, each with fifty-foot lengths of hose designed to reach every part of the vessel and connected at all times. Alarm boxes placed around the ship to be rung at regular intervals would register in the pilothouse. The electrical system would be unmatched, supplying forty-five hundred lights. An automatic signal board on the bridge would control the ship's signal lights, whose lamps would be in duplicate; if one lamp failed, the other would automatically light and register the failure in the pilothouse. An electric whistle device would also automatically blow the fog signal at regular intervals during thick weather. Five hundred telephones would allow every traveler communication with the ship's staff, other passengers, or anyone in the city when docked. The wireless system would include a battery plant, which would allow operation of the system for six hours, should a power failure occur. Lifesaving equipment would meet government requirements (eighteen metal lifeboats and more than the number of life rafts and life preservers required by the United States inspection service). The vessel would be supplied with a thirty-two-inch searchlight, the largest on the Great Lakes. A triple whistle on the forward funnel would have a twenty-six-, a ten-, and six-inch-long bells. To assist in critical steering maneuvers, besides an after rudder, the steamer would be fitted with a bow rudder controlled by a separate steam steering engine. In the center of the broad, many windowed pilothouse would be three large steering wheels in tandem, further unspoken testimony of her greatness.

It is hard today to comprehend what it was like to have the largest vessel in your world under construction in your backyard. One could hardly compare it to the building of a skyscraper or some other confined or cordoned-off building site. Although construction of the vessel was not open for public viewing, the well-advertised project acted like a magnet that attracted the eyes and ears of those surrounding the work. After all, this was to be the largest side-wheeler in the world! Then, too, any novice could estimate the immense scale of the task by merely watching the hundreds upon hundreds of skilled craftsmen from every line of work flowing to and from the yard each day as the giant took shape. Most astonishing was the forty-some acres of material and equipment stockpiled for the job. The immense stacks of steel of every size and shape, stuck here and there like pieces of a gigantic puzzle, certainly gave no clue that the end

The *Seeandbee*'s three big steering wheels. (Dossin Great Lakes Museum)

The *Seeandbee* sits on the ways ready for launch.

product would someday be the sleek-lined vessel everyone was talking about.

There lay her 78′, three-sectioned, 120-ton main shaft, one of the largest forgings ever made. This shining object of engineering perfection was 29³/4″ at its widest diameter and had a 11³/4″ hole throughout its length. The main shafts of the battleship *Texas*,[5] which were also made by the Midvale Steel Company, Midvale, Pennsylvania, were minuscule in comparison. The pile of material for her paddlewheels alone seemed ample enough to erect a small building. From this stock would come two, 33-foot-diameter paddlewheels each weighing a hundred tons. They would each hold eleven steel paddles/buckets that would measure 14′ 10″ long x 5′ 1″ wide x 1³/8″ thick. The iron forgings and cast steel makeup of these wheels were especially designed to withstand the severe ice conditions often encountered on the spring runs to Buffalo. The six 14-foot-diameter x 10¹/2-foot boilers, the low- and high-pressure cylinders (the largest on any Great Lakes steamer), and connecting rods would have a combined weight of 492 tons! The two, sixty-five hundred-pound anchors, seemingly stout enough to check a much larger vessel, took up a good portion of the yard. Coiled nearby was 1,110 feet of 2¼" steel chain cable, the snakelike mass a wonder in itself to visualize.

The average enthusiast seldom has the opportunity to view, up close, the construction of "a floating city" or see all the material, equipment, and accoutrements necessary to build an enormous vessel. The details of her majesty and magnitude were therefore described in the advertisement for this grand lady. She would have 510 staterooms and 24 parlors and would accommodate fifteen hundred passengers, equal to the accommodations offered by any of the larger hotels in the country. She would have a carrying capacity of nearly six thousand people. . .no wonder she was called a city! (By comparison, the eleven hundred-foot nuclear aircraft carrier USS *Enterprise* carries a crew of fifty-five hundred people). Her seven decks would offer a truly majestic sight. From the top these were to be: the dome deck, upper deck, gallery deck, promenade deck, main deck, top tank deck, and orlop deck.

Launch day for the "giant" was particularly thrilling. About three thousand people were there, including a hundred special guests, most of whom would be brought from Detroit aboard the steamer *Britannia*. Strange as it was, the name of this new vessel was still a secret. The great ship stood there on the greased ways, which were a mere fifteen feet wider than her beam. High on the bow, where her name would normally be found, hung a large placard inscribed with an enormous question mark. Only before the last-

A placard with a question mark covers the name at the launching of the *Seeandbee*. (Great Lakes Historical Society)

minute preparations were made ready for launch did there appear on the bow flagstaff a fluttering blue pennant with the name *Seeandbee* on it. A contest, which had been held by the owners, offered a cash prize of fifty dollars for the most appropriate name. Many in the crowd and on the *Britannia* were among the twenty-seven hundred contestants to offer a name for the vessel. A few with binoculars spotted the unusual name first and passed the word to others as disappointed sighs reverberated throughout the spectators. Miss May Knight from Cleveland was the lucky girl. Her idea was taken from the names of the owners of the company (C&B), the cities between which the vessel would travel, and the sound, she thought, of a rather harmonious title. The name stood out from all the rest. Another girl, submitting an identical name, but later than Miss Knight's suggestion, would receive a second prize of thirty dollars. "Surely that can't be the real name for it" was uttered by many throughout the crowd. In their usual forward manner, some attending members of the marine community were overheard saying that the name sounded too much like a breakfast food!

Just before noon that ninth day of November 1912, the sponsor, Miss Eleanor Moodey, from Painesville, Ohio, bedecked in a large cascade corsage of fresh flowers, cracked a silver-encased bottle of wine across the sharp prow exactly on the number "seven" depth marking. At this instant, Frank Jeffreys, the yard superintendent, swelling with the great pride of the moment, gave the signal to release the vessel. Sliding into the water with both ease and great force, the pristine hulk caused a gigantic roaring splash that was drowned out in the cheers of the throng. According to the vesselmen in attendance, because the *Seeandbee* had been christened by striking the "lucky number seven," she would therefore be "a most fortunate ship." A luncheon and dance followed the festivities.

Fitting-out of the *Seeandbee* took place during the winter of 1912-13. Like most vessels, "the launch" is often mistakenly considered to signify the completion of the ship. For purposes of the overall "look" of the vessel, it is just the beginning. It represents only the christening of the basic hull with little, if any, superstructure in place. Once the launch determined that the *Seeandbee* was truly the sound and secure vessel that is was designed to be, the fitting-out stage of construction began. Then came the army of rough and finish carpenters, electricians, pipe fitters, decorators, painters, carpet layers, and a score of other specialists and technicians to build her cabins, staterooms, and service areas, add the detail mouldings, create the decorative touches, clean and polish. Already in training was another equally large regiment of the ship's crew, stewards, waiters, bellhops, cooks, housekeepers, and other service personnel.

After the long and seemingly endless list of known tasks and tedious odd jobs was finished, the absolute completion of the beautiful lady was at hand. Finally the magnificent end product, the architect's fulfilled dream, her beauty visualized only on paper just months ago, was now real and there to behold. Amazingly, less than one year and two months had elapsed from the first day of her contract until she was ready for service.

The key to marine interior decorator Louis O. Keil's grand theme for the *Seeandbee* was surroundings of "rich simplicity." His heralded accomplishments included the grandiose interior decorating of the Hudson River day liners and the Detroit and Cleveland Navigation steamers. Spaciously equal to a large hotel, in the lobby of the *Seeandbee* passengers got their first impression of the vessel. Surrounded in rich paneled mahogany inlaid with other woods, a passenger could look to the ceiling and appreciate the gleaming bronze ceiling fixtures and pillar supports, which offered the warmth of simple elegance. Conveniently, this large entrance lobby also contained the purser's and steward's offices, parcel and baggage rooms, a lunch counter and telephone booths. The bottom of the wide, grand stairway, which led to the promenade deck, had an enclosed vestibule with sliding doors that could shut off a deadly draft in case of fire—another safety consideration.

The pleasant atmosphere of the main dining room, located aft of the lobby, offered dinner guests a beautiful view of the passing panorama. Though seating 170 people at once in mostly an open arrangement, there were also bay window alcoves that offered some privacy. A twenty-four-foot banquet room on the starboard side and two private dining rooms on the port side served guests for more private affairs. Sheffield silver candelabra and wall bracket lighting fixtures set the perfect flair for the surroundings of mahogany and white enamel. After dinner, guests could congregate in the Old English style tavern beneath the dining room.

Once again in the lobby, a flight up the wide stairs in the vestibule brought you to the nearly four hundred-foot-long main saloon on the promenade deck. The flower booths, observation room, ladies and mens writing rooms, and bookstore offered passengers a quiet retreat and necessities to

The *Seeandbee* was the only four-stacker on the Great Lakes. (Great Lakes Historical Society)

help pass the time. The ceilings in both the forward and after sections, along with the large cross-bulkhead panels at the stairway landings, embraced large murals that set an exquisite decorative theme in an otherwise simple decor. The framed-in works of art made one feel that they were viewing the paintings hung in a collector's mansion rather than on a ship. Special parlors bordering the main saloon, named after officials of the C&B company, contained twin brass beds, a divan, tables, dressers, chairs, and mirrors, along with a private bath and balcony. Treated with the utmost refined decor, some of the parlors were paneled in silk, brocade, and finely embroidered curtains.

Up one level, the gallery deck included a ladies drawing room at the aft end and a writing room forward with cabins beside each area and amidships. Again, carrying the simple yet refined decor, the color scheme for this deck was gray, ivory, and white. There were built-in walnut seats in the aft portion of the ladies drawing room along with comfortably stuffed chairs and rose-colored ceiling fixtures.

Expected to be one of the most popular areas on the ship, the lounge, on the upper deck, was treated with an extra special theme. Finished in fumed oak, the designs painted directly on wall and ceiling wood panels created an almost cathedral-like atmosphere. More paintings set in huge panels surrounding the stack casings, which reached from floor to ceiling, displayed yet another tasteful touch. Many small bays on both sides of the room made eating the refreshments served there, along with the passing view, all the more enjoyable. The asbestolith floor, divided into squares by shining brass strips, resembled a floor treatment you would expect to see in a king's throne room. At the bottom of the arched ceiling were small skylights that added more natural light to the comfortable setting. The atrium, or court room, adjoining the staterooms on this deck carried a Pompeian theme with its rich colors, painted ceilings, and bronze torch lighting fixtures.

One of the most beautiful design features of the vessel were the elegant balconies on each level. From the orchestra platform at the after end of the main saloon and forward of the ladies drawing room, the music could easily be heard in the main saloon, the drawing room, and the atrium on the upper decks.

It was time for the grand lady to go to work. She left Detroit on this maiden trip June 19, 1913, at 8:35 A.M. amid a clamor of salutes from nearby vessels and the cheers of those who came to see her off. This bon voyage, however, was

The *Seeandbee* downbound in the Detroit River. (Dossin Great Lakes Museum)

The *Seeandbee* in a fresh following wind, her decks full of passengers. (Great Lakes Historical Museum)

The *Seeandbee* glides to her dock as awed passengers gape at her majestic stature. (Dossin Great Lakes Museum)

mild in comparison to the reception she received at Cleveland. Even before she was inside the breakwater, thousands of well-wishers, gathered on rooftops and any other available wharf vantage point, greeted the *Seeandbee* as she arrived that afternoon. At 10:00 that evening she departed for her maiden Buffalo run.

Far different from her initial ebullient reception was the lukewarm passenger trade. She was barely broken in as World War I began in 1914. Along with the *Titanic* disaster, the loss of 1,000 lives in the sinking of the *Empress of Ireland* in the St. Lawrence River May 29, 1914, the loss of 1,198 lives in the sinking of the *Lusitania* by a German submarine May 7, 1915, the tragic loss of 812 lives on the *Eastland* in Chicago Harbor July 24, 1915, and a sharply reduced operating schedule as a result of the Seaman's Act had severe dampening effects on her ability to realize any appreciated earnings from 1914 to 1918. The Seaman's Act alone smothered her earning capability. The act restricted her carrying capacity before May 15 and after September 15, allowing only ninety days of mild profit. The three-year period from 1919 to 1922 stood out as the only time that she could nearly realize her full earning capability. Beginning in 1923, a gradual but steady decline was evident. In 1926 this developed into the tailspin of consistent loss that was to stay with her throughout her career. If the dark cloud of the war, marine disasters, and the Seaman's Act weren't fully responsible for the decline, then the competition she faced from the automobile, buses, trains, and planes surely helped. Along with fall cruises from Cleveland to the Soo in 1921 and 1922, and six out-of-season upper lake cruises, she maintained the Buffalo run until 1931. In 1932 she was absolutely idle and did not run at all.

As a passenger on the *Seeandbee*, your experience was filled with fun and happiness. Other than possibly noticing fewer passengers aboard, you would have had little knowledge of a company in trouble. Your only cares were left at the dock. You could board the big vessel in Buffalo and depart at 8:00 P.M. for a seven-day trip to Chicago and back. For this one-way, all-expenses-paid trip, the 1938 fare of $42.50 gave you a modest inside room. A stateroom with twin beds, veranda, bath, and toilet would cost $79.50. For an additional ten dollars you could take your car along. A travel-now and pay-later plan allowed you up to a year to pay as little as $5.50 a month. After an exquisite eight-course dinner featuring broiled Lake Erie whitefish, grilled spring lamb chops, or fried chicken with all the trimmings, you could retire to the ballroom where the nightly "Seeandbee Revue" floor show, with Tony Cabot and his orchestra, could help you get acquainted with other passengers. Tommy Nesbit at the organ or a changing host of other professional entertainers would supply plenty of evening enjoyment. If you were more interested in watching the ship's progress as she steamed westward in Lake Erie, you might have been

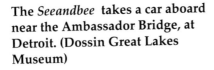

The *Seeandbee* takes a car aboard near the Ambassador Bridge, at Detroit. (Dossin Great Lakes Museum)

lucky enough to experience the enchantment of seeing another eastbound liner, with all lights ablaze, pass your vessel nearby. Sleeping on the hundred-foot beam (at the time the fourth widest in the world) held a special pleasure and a most smooth sailing experience. To accompany the strains of the orchestra faintly audible in your stateroom, you were "hummed" to sleep by the soothing sound of the ship's churning paddlewheels deep within your pillow.

Next morning everyone would be anxious to down the hearty breakfast and participate in the array of planned activities, which included miniature horse races, Ping Pong, shuffleboard, exercising, and cards. Plenty of comfortable deck chairs were waiting for those content with daydreaming in the sun. Arriving in Detroit at noon, you were amazed how the crew sprang into action with a hubbub of docking activity at the busy wharf. Because the ship sailed that afternoon, a brief walk to nearby shops was all you had time for. You certainly did not want to miss the ship or the tea dance at 5:00 P.M. Dancing for prizes and musical games would be big hits with most everyone. Was it by chance that you once again met that special person you saw at the dance? A spell was cast on both of you by the gold evening colors spreading their majesty along the winding St. Clair River. It was, therefore, romantically decided that the rest of the trip would be be spent together. Winding up the day as new members of the "Owls Club" in the tavern or the lounge offered further special moments with your new sweetheart. As you sailed northward into Lake Huron, the full moon's sparkle on the lake made a perfect last view before retiring.

Passengers promenade on the *Seeandbee*'s deck for exercise and appetite.

85

With cordial hospitality you were spoiled with another bountiful breakfast as you sailed the North Channel of Georgian Bay. Deck games with special prizes followed and quickly captured the spotlight. Arriving at the Soo after lunch, you were allowed an hour to visit the locks and the city of Sault Ste Marie. Sailing again at 2:30 P.M., there were bridge or keno tournaments and another tea dance to help you wile away the time. Many passengers would be busy planning their 13½-hour stay at Mackinac Island, the "Bermuda of the North." While the ship stayed at the island, you could join the festivities at the Grand Hotel, or enjoy the serene and quiet of the quaint island. Leaving at 10:00 the next morning, you were especially excited to get on with the next leg of your trip. For a scenic off-Lake Michigan and unusual diversion, the *Seeandbee* would sail through Green Bay, being the only liner to offer such a treat. Hundreds of camera bugs would try to capture the magnificent sunset; others would enjoy the evening at Capt. Allan Strachan's grand dinner and dance. As you sailed toward Chicago, this festive farewell party, complete with streamers, flags, noisemakers, and balloons in Mardi Gras fashion, would be in full force in the dining salon. The special captain's toast bid farewell to those departing in Chicago. Sparkling with the merriment of a New Year's celebration, but punctuated with tender, romantic good-byes, this party was like what you might find taking place at a farewell event on the *Queen Mary*. At breakfast, as the last addresses of new-found sweethearts were exchanged, you realized you had until evening to see the "Windy City." With departing time set to

The *Seeandbee* is backed from her slip nearly full of passengers.

take advantage of the usual beautiful sunset, you started the return voyage, retracing the upbound legs to arrive in Buffalo before 8:00 P.M., some 2¹/₂ days later.

From 1933 to 1938 the *Seeandbee* was involved in a weekly cruise service. Chartered to the Chicago firm of T. J. McGuire & Associates in 1939 and 1940, she was sold to that organization (which became known as the Cleveland and Buffalo Transit Company of Illinois) in March 1941 for $135,000.

Hitler's terror statements of dreaded attacks against the Atlantic convoy supply ships to Europe continued to shock the world. With each terse radio news broadcast an announcement that we were at war seemed inevitable. Busy training fighter pilots, the few aircraft carriers we had needed protection from the precious few escort ships. This foreboding predicament resulted in the brilliant suggestion of an Atlantic merchant marine sailor, John J. Manley. His idea became one of the most significant reasons for our World War II victory. It involved converting an existing Great Lakes excursion liner into an aircraft carrier for training pilots on the Great Lakes. Timely as it was, the idea was welcomed and soon presented to the higher echelons of the navy for study. The attack on Pearl Harbor by the Japanese on December 7, 1941, paved the way to go ahead with the project at an accelerated pace. Because he was familiar with Great Lakes navigation, and because he knew the *Seeandbee* like his own ship, Manley, who by this time was a newly volunteered U.S. Navy seaman, was placed in charge of the conversion. Even though the would-be, makeshift carrier would

Smoke billows aft from the *Seeandbee* as viewed on the boat deck.

be unarmed, unescorted, and a thousand miles from sea, the scheme seemed perfect.

The *Seeandbee* was requisitioned by the United States government on March 12, 1942, and bought by the navy for $756,560. Her superstructure was taken off down to the main deck level at the American Shipbuilding Company plant in Cleveland. On May 10, after the hull was towed to Buffalo, the second phase of the conversion began in earnest. At first only about 125 workers pored over the task. But it was soon realized that if the 120-day completion deadline was to be met, more workers were necessary. Her centered smoke-stacks had to be moved to the starboard side and steel framework had to be erected to support the three-inch Douglas fir flight deck. A small "island" surrounding the stacks and housing the navigation bridge and observation tower would offer similarity to her larger counterparts. There would be no hangar deck to store planes on and no catapults to launch them; consequently, all takeoffs would require the entire flight deck. She would have an eight-wire arresting system, the amazing apparatus that caught the

The *Seeandbee* with just a few passengers aboard. (Dossin Great Lakes Museum)

The *Seeandbee* under U.S. Navy guard just before her carrier conversion.

A view of the port quarter of the USS *Wolverine*. Note that the radar on her upper mast was blotted out in this wartime photograph. (Courtesy U.S. Naval Institute)

landing aircraft's hook. Amid the project, the war effort in full swing, with patriotism and productivity at an all-time high, twelve hundred men worked on the job twenty-four hours a day to complete the project in three months and two days! The conversion cost was $1,935,343.

Pilots were desperately needed. The unusual-looking carrier, named after the first iron ship of the navy the USS *Wolverine*,[6] with the official navy designation of IX-64[7] was commissioned, rushed through her trials, and sailed to Chicago to go "into action" by the 22nd of August 1942. The jury-rigged carrier's flight deck was only twenty-seven feet from the water compared with the seventy-foot height of the bigger carriers. Measuring 550' x 103' wide, the flight deck's size and recovery attributes would teach pilots, it was reported, to land on a lily pad.[8] With little more than a month of practical training at the Naval Air Station, Grosse Ile, Michigan, or Glenview Naval Air Station, north of Chicago, student fliers were sent out to qualify by completing eight landings and takeoffs on the decks of the *Wolverine*. At top speed she could create nineteen knots of wind over her deck. This was enough for the slower aircraft, but for the faster F4U Corsairs and F6F Hellcats, a combination of carrier speed and wind speed was necessary. Thus, when heavy winds sprang up on the lake, the Glenview station was alerted so that the faster aircraft could "scramble" into flight for their landings. Because the *Wolverine* had no storage area for aircraft, they were all stationed at Glenview.

A peculiar problem facing pilots approaching the carrier was the belching, coal-fired smoke trailing over the recovery area of the flight deck. It was quickly discovered, however, that by steering the ship with the wind five or ten degrees on her port bow, the heavy smoke would drift off over her starboard quarter and away from recovery operations. This slight, manufactured crosswind made landings tricky, but when winds recorded as high as forty-one knots (June 12,

1943) crossed the deck, the landings were even more treacherous. What a sight this must have been! Imagine the big carrier puffing heavy smoke and plowing through the sea creating a spectacular wash from her paddlewheels with her landing signal officer desperately guiding the rookie pilots aboard! Action on the flight deck was filled with electrified excitement that also provided valuable experience. The crash barrier, a weblike net strung across the flight deck to "catch" disabled aircraft or those that failed to grab the arresting wire, prevented their travel farther down the deck. The *Wolverine* offered many crash barrier crews this "hands-on" training.

The first landing at 1010 hours on August 26, 1942, by Lieutenant Boyers, as might be expected, was anticipated and watched by many with bated breath. Would this unorthodox carrier do the job? Most likely Boyers was the top airman of his class and was ushered quickly into reality by being the very first and honored pilot to land on the new carrier. Fortunately, the embarrassing incident that followed did not reflect the future to any great extent because this first aircraft crashed the number one barrier because it did not have its hook down!

There were plenty of mishaps, but they were greatly outweighed by successes. On September 17, only twenty-two days from the beginning of operations, Ensign Harding made the one thousandth landing! The *Wolverine* was so successful that the Detroit & Cleveland Navigation Company steamer *Greater Buffalo* was quickly requisitioned by the government, converted in the same manner, and commissioned into the navy as the USS *Sable* (IX-81) May 8, 1943, to join in the project on Lake Michigan. The first casualty was logged October 21, when an F-4, piloted by Ens. Fred Morgan, crashed and sank in eighty-five feet of water. Ensign Morgan's body was not recovered.

On Navy Day, October 25, 1942, this NBC radio broadcast was conducted live from the deck of the USS *Wolverine*:

> "Today, the Navy's aviation arm is being expanded at top speed. Ships are being converted into carriers, and new carriers are sliding-down the ways. Deadly Navy planes are pouring-from the production line. To man these carriers and planes, thousands of keen determined young Americans are now being trained. For the first time since this war began, we take you aboard a carrier underway to show you this air combat training in action."
>
> (Sounds of alarm bell and airplane engines warming up) . . .
> "Every man aboard this carrier is on the alert, at battle stations! She's nosing into the wind! About to launch the planes which are warming up on the flight deck! Scouting planes from this carrier

are already in the air, and they are presumed to have sought and to have found the enemy. Let's listen in on the radio loud speaker and her the pilot scouting plane report. . ." (Sound of airplane engine and static):

". . .DOG. . .BAKER. . .ZED. . .FROM SAIL RIGHT WING. . .ENEMY TASK FORCE SIGHTED. . .TWO CARRIERS, THREE HEAVY CRUISERS. . .BEARING ONE THREE ZERO. . .DISTANCE EIGHT ZERO MILES FROM POINT ZED. . .ON COURSE ONE TWO ZERO. . .SPEED ONE SEVEN. . .ENEMY PLANES FROM CARRIERS ARE CIRCLING OVER FORCE. . .(SOUND OF AIRCRAFT DIVING). . .FROM SAIL RIGHT WING. . .THAT IS ALL. . ."

"The enemy is sighted; the moment for which this proud ship was built, for which these proud fighting men were trained. Down in the ready room, the carrier pilots sit waiting for their orders. Let's listen to the carrier's telephone circuit to hear the Air Plot Officer assign specific tasks to the squadron leaders. The information which is being compiled is being written on a black board (sound of aircraft overhead) in front of the pilots, and the pilots are entering this information on their flight logs. In full flying gear, they sit tense and silent, plotting their courses. Now the boys are scrambling up from the ready room on the double, through the companion ways and up the ladders to the flight deck (sound of footsteps climbing ladder) where their planes face into the wind! From our position here topside, high on the flight control bridge, we can see the plane captains welcoming the pilots with big grins telling them that their planes are ready to go. (Wailing warning horn—planes passing overhead) The Flight Control Officer here beside me speaks into the microphone of the bullhorn which can be heard above every other noise on the ship. Most of the pilots are in their planes by now, the plane captains stand to one side, ready to pull the chocks from the wheels. Many of these men (sound of plane diving overhead) are giving the 'thumb up' to the dispatcher who stands on a platform from which he waves the planes into the air! (Voice from loudspeaker updates bearings of approaching enemy task force.) And now the pilots are pushing their cockpits closed! One by one (sound of planes passing overhead) they are giving the 'thumbs up' signal down to the officer, the Flight Deck Officer. . .he's returning the signal! Now the Flight Deck Officer is giving the O.K. signal to the Flight Control Officer beside me up here on the flight control deck! (Voice from loudspeaker. . .'planes are ready to be launched, Captain') The Flight Control Officer has notified the Commanding Officer that all planes are ready to be launched! (Sound of aircraft overhead.) The Captain is giving the order to take off! And now the dispatcher is waving the planes into the air. . .there they go! (Sound of aircraft taking off nearby.) Those pilots are on their own now, their months of training, their devotion to duty focused on one objective. . .VICTORY!"

"After such training exercises as you have just heard, the Navy and Marine Corps pilots go directly to battle areas. So far in this war, they have earned our nation's highest praise and the enemy's deepest respect. They have established new traditions which will become a part of our Navy's history."

Duty on the carrier was particularly harsh. Anyone who has felt the doldrums of a hundred-degree summer day or the minus-forty-below wind chill of a November gale on Lake Michigan could imagine the misery of standing watch on the *Wolverine*. The log is full of assorted punishments, from restricted liberty to five days of bread and water for shirking duty, to being AOL (absent over leave). Because the *Wolverine* had to steam back and forth to her anchorage in Chicago Harbor to coal up and replenish stores, liberty there was a problem. Despite the obstacles of low morale, of the torrid summer heat, and the most severe winter in thirty-nine years (1942), it is truly remarkable how this operation not only was a success, but far surpassed all expectations. From August 26, 1942, to November 7, 1945, there were 113 barrier crashes and 38 other on-deck crashes or mishaps involving aircraft damage.[9] The highest wind across her deck was fifty-eight knots on July 27, 1944. Thirty-six aircraft were lost and sunk in Lake Michigan. Three fatalities were recorded during this time; two of these airmen were never found.

A big boost to morale came on April 26, 1943, at 1200 hours when Col. Charles A. Lindbergh landed aboard in a J-17 to observe carrier landings. On June 11, 1943, only 289 days since her operations began, Lt. C. E. Roemer made the ten thousandth landing aboard her flight deck. In total, the *Wolverine* logged seventy thousand successful landings and takeoffs, qualifying over twelve thousand pilots. It is well agreed that the carriers did the most to help win the war in the Pacific; it could also be stated that the *Wolverine*, in training many of the heroes who flew the missions, was crucial to winning the war in that theater.

The last log entry for flight operations was Tuesday, September 18, 1945. Void of any flowery writing or emotion, the log simply reads, "Flight operations completed." The proud *Wolverine* was decommissioned at 1037 hours, November 7, 1945, and sold shortly after for scrap for $46,789. As she was being dismantled, many of her pilots who lived to see that day, as well as the ghosts of those who fell in action, surely must have bowed their heads at the passing of this gallant lady.

5. THE *HURON LIGHTSHIP*

Sweeping antipodes
That broom away the dark,
Painting the mural gloom
With cosmic-stroking brush!

Michael J. Moakler,
"Lone Selfless Anchorite"

If you have ever stood safely on a gale-swept shore and watched the piercing beacon of a lightship casting its magic through the darkness or heard a distant moaning foghorn, you might have witnessed the romantic yet eerie enchantment of these noble sentries. If, on the other hand, you see the light from your ship as you grope desperately through a storm searching for that tiny speck of light that marks the right course, the welcome sight is one of profound relief, all romance aside.

Lightships, or mobile lighthouses, provided the same service as lighthouses, except that the duty on lightships was much more hazardous. Being "out there" on open water in a storm or in fog as ships steered directly at you presented the constant danger of being run down or blown away at the mercy of the gale. Convincing examples of these hazards occurred during the storms of 1913 when *Lightship No. 61* was blown helplessly from her moorings to become steadfast again two miles east and two miles south of her station. Unable to return to his station without orders, the keeper of the lightship stayed put, which resulted in the steamer *Matthew Andrews* going aground on Corsica Shoal. *Lightship No. 82* off Point Abino in Lake Erie stood on station and was lost in the same storms with all hands.[10]

The last of some twenty-two lightships on the Great Lakes and one of the last to serve in the United States, the *Huron Lightship* occupies a corner of history. The tiny vessel kept ships off Corsica Shoals and honorably guided sailors into the St. Clair River for thirty-six years.[11]

The ninety-seven-foot long, twenty-four-foot beam, steel lightship, first designated number 103, which some said resembled a water bug, was built for the United States

An early photo of the *Huron Lightship No. 61*. (Dossin Great Lakes Museum)

Lighthouse Service in 1920 at Morris Heights, New York, at a cost of $126,428. After her commissioning in 1921, she came directly to Milwaukee, and at first served as a relief vessel for several other lakes lightships. At this time her hull color was a bright red with white letters.

The vessel had a thirteen thousand-candlepower beacon that could send a beam of light about fourteen miles; it had a crew of eleven. The lower Lake Huron lightship station/location, six miles north of Port Huron, was established in 1893 when it was decided that a manned light vessel would be more dependable than the gas-lit buoy that marked the shoals before this time. Three different lightships would carry the name *Huron*. The first one, *Lightship No. 61*, served this station from September 1893 until 1921. *Lightship No 96* served there from 1921 to 1934.

From 1924 to 1932 the vessel served as the *Relief* at Gray's Reef in the shipping channel west of the Straits of Mackinac; and from 1933 to 1934 she was stationed at Manitou Shoals in Lake Michigan. In 1934 she took up her position on Lake Huron and her hull color was changed from red to black, the color of which identified the side of the ship channel that the vessel marked. She would be known from now on as the only United States lightship having a black hull. Her exact position was marked on the Lake Huron charts, enabling mariners on passing vessels to check their radio direction finders for accuracy. During thick weather, her radio beacon would continuously send out a series of three dashes, for a full minute, every three minutes.

When the Coast Guard took over the lighthouse service

The *Huron Lightship*

in 1939, the *Huron Lightship* became the *Wal-526*. During World War II, she would have the distinction of being the only lightship to remain on station for the duration of the war. From 1940 on, the *Huron* was the only lightship on the Great Lakes. During a 1949 refit her old boilers were replaced with two diesel engines along with a radio beacon, radar, and up-to-date fog-signal equipment.

The two-year tour of duty aboard the lightship, though not laborious or frustrating in calm weather, was "hell to pay" during bad. Her five thousand-pound anchor would keep her steadfast, but it was always a rough ride in stormy weather. The crew's duties were ever constant in good weather or bad. Usually six men were on watch at a time, and her foghorn and beacon had to be kept running and in tip-top condition. Off-watch sleep came hard during the long-lasting (sometimes thirty-six hours) heavy fog that often invaded the area. Reverberating through every cranny of the ship, it was said that the foghorn, after blasting non-stop for these long periods, would totally exhaust the crew, for there was no place on the small vessel to hide from the drone.

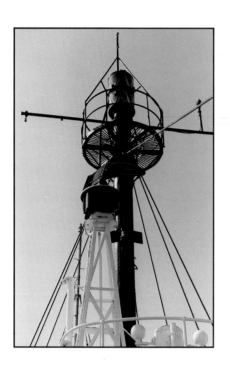

The *Huron Lightship*'s mast and light beacon.

Provisions were stocked at the beginning of the season and replenished with a supply boat twice a week; the chow matched that found on any Great Lakes ship. A small but cozy ward room offered off-duty crew members the chance to play cards, study, write letters, or watch television. A twenty-five-foot motor launch made one feel not too far from "the world" back on shore.

The Coast Guard, estimating the lightship would cost $105,500 annually to operate, determined that some $87,000 could be saved yearly by replacing the lightship with a battery-powered, lighted, horn buoy. The *Huron Lightship*, after forty-nine years of service on the lakes, was decommissioned August 25, 1970. The new buoy, about three thousand feet north of the *Huron's* old station, would flash a white light every four seconds at three hundred candlepower with a range of 8.8 miles. Its fog signal would blast every thirty seconds with a range of one mile with its radar reflector operating at a range of 6 miles.[12] A radio beacon would be stationed at the Fort Gratiot Light Station.

How many mariners had she guided to safety? How many pleasure boaters, after seeing her, felt that "finally safe" feeling after coming in from a storm-swept Lake Huron, to say nothing of those countless shipwatchers and lakefront dwellers who took her for granted for so many years? Her nickname,"Old-Bee-Oh," coined from the sound

of her foghorn, became a warm spot in the hearts of many. She stood for something more than just a lightship. To those who braved the long swim out to her station, she was an old friend. She signified tranquility during an endless summer. To those who went out to her in rowboats as the moon rose off the lake, she was cupid himself, aglow in a sea of sparkling silver.

So endeared was the *Huron Lightship* to the many thousands who knew her that when the people of Port Huron, Michigan, learned that she might be given to the city of Grand Haven, Michigan, they began a fight to win their sweetheart back. If some other city should have the *Huron*, Grand Haven was a prime candidate, for the annual Coast Guard festival is held there. Port Huron citizens, however, would not give in. Some four thousand schoolchildren wrote to Washington, D. C., pleading for "their" lightship to stay in Port Huron, and citizens approved a $400,000 proposal to pay for the required seawall improvements. The Coast Guard, swayed by the city's sentiment over the vessel, finally gave it to Port Huron. And so, acquired by the city through direct approval of area citizens, the *Huron Lightship* now permanently rests at Pine Grove Park for all to love and cherish and remember her noble and friendly career.

Ships are referred to as "ladies," and the *Huron Lightship* is no exception. Another lady, Ida Lewis, was one of the very

The *Huron Lightship* as seen in her later thirty-six-year career. (Dossin Great Lakes Museum)

few *lady* lighthouse keepers in the United States. She inherited her job from her father, who kept the lonely light on Lime Rock inside of Newport Harbor, Rhode Island. From rowing her heavy lapstrake boat to the endless chore of maintaining the beacon, her tough duties included rescuing eighteen mariners, some of whom she had rowed several miles in gale winds to save! Shortly before her retirement, she became the first woman to receive a medal for bravery along with a commemorative letter from the president of the United States. Her lasting memorial, the Ida Lewis Yacht Club flag bears a lighthouse on a field of eighteen stars.

The five thousand-pound bell anchor on the *Huron Lightship*.

The historic vessel, the *Huron Lightship*, at her permanent dock at Pinegrove Park, Port Huron, Michigan.

6. THE *AQUARAMA*

Sure! The *Aquarama*. I remember that boat!
Of course! She was the neatest thing afloat.
But she hit a lotta docks, for heaven's sakes,
And in her spare time she cruised the lakes.

One of eleven deep-draft transport vessels constructed during the latter part of World War II, the *Marine Star*, a C-4, SB2 Type 10 cargo ship, was built by the Sun Shipbuilding Company of Chester, Pennsylvania. Just a young lady, she had logged only 100,000 miles from the time she went into service until the government put her in mothballs after the war. In 1950 she was purchased by Sand Products of Detroit along with another C-4, the *Marine Robin*, later converted to the ore carrier *Joseph L. Thompson*, and a C-5, the *Marine Angel*, later converted to the self-unloader *McKee Sons*.

The grand heyday of excursion steamboating on the Great Lakes was nearly at its end. It was a time when people were sadly watching the last of the passenger liners being scrapped or burned. About all that remained in operation were the *North* and *South American*. Max McKee, president of Sand Products, however, had what he thought was a fresh idea. He believed that the automobile, one of the primary reasons for the passenger trade decline in the first place, was clogging roads to the extent that people would again welcome the opportunity to take their cars with them on excursions between Cleveland and Detroit. The trip would save a motorist 180 miles in a shortcut across Lake Erie. To prove his point he would spend millions converting the *Marine Star* into the finest liner ever. Just as thousands of Great Lakes steamboat enthusiasts still believe, it was his steadfast belief that the traditional appeal of the "boat ride" was very much alive. He further believed that he would be fully operational to cash in on an expected explosion of the excursion trade with this modern vessel, and possibly others, when the St. Lawrence Seaway opened.

The conversion on the *Marine Star* began in 1952 at the

The C-5 cargo vessel, then unnamed and nearing completion at Muskegon, Michigan, in 1955.

Todd Shipyards in Brooklyn; the original superstructure was removed leaving only the engines and the basic hull. A year later the hull was towed down the Atlantic coast and into the Gulf of Mexico to New Orleans where it was fitted with pontoons for the long trip up the Mississippi River, through the Illinois waterway, and across Lake Michigan to Muskegon, Michigan. Even with the superstructure removed, it was still, at 55½ feet, the tallest vessel to pass through the waterway and negotiate passage beneath the stationary bridges along the way. After five years of architectural planning and engineering, it was there in Muskegon in 1954 that the second stage of the conversion would take place. Having secured bids for the project from various shipyards and contractors, the owners decided on an unprecedented dockside conversion instead of having the work done at conventional shipyards, which were too crowded anyway. They would be their own general contractor and subcontract work to local firms, many of which, it was thought, had little or no experience in that line of work.

By creating the look of an ocean liner, she would indeed be something new on the lakes. Additionally, she would be the first new liner on the lakes in twenty years. Only the great 535-foot steamers *Greater Detroit* and *Greater Buffalo*, of the then defunct Detroit & Cleveland Navigation Company, would have exceeded her length by fifteen feet. However, with a gross tonnage of about 11,000 she was larger, compared with their tonnage of 7,739. Almost a city block long, the 520-foot, 71-foot 6-inch beam vessel would accommodate 2,500 passengers and 165 autos. In taking a complete tour of her nine decks, two of which were for cars, one would cover two miles. She would displace 10,600 tons, or about the same as a navy cruiser. Her oil-fired engines would produce 10,000 horsepower that would propel a single 21½-foot, 10-ton bronze screw to offer a cruising speed of twenty-two miles per hour. Her 22-inch-diameter drive shaft was the largest on the lakes.

100

The *Aquarama*

The work on the vessel was described as the most extensive ship conversion ever attempted at a Great Lakes dock. In May 1954 Sand Products leased the ship to the Michigan Ohio Navigation Company, which announced the proposed passenger service between Cleveland and Detroit. People around Muskegon watched with amazement as the drab hull was gradually, but systematically, changed into a "fair lady" right before their eyes. A lucky Detroit contestant won a thousand dollars for coming up with the perfect name for the revitalized ship. Taken from the word *aqua* for water and "rama" for a good display, the name *Aquarama* was chosen to emphasize the modern grandeur of the vessel. Construction delays on docking facilities at Cleveland would prevent the new vessel from entering service in 1955 as planned. In July of that year, the completed pristine vessel, built at a cost of $8 million, was towed out through the Lake Michigan channel at Muskegon, as an estimated crowd of ten to fifteen thousand spectators lined the shore and in a flotilla of small craft to watch her depart. To show the lady off, she was docked at the Navy Pier in Chicago where visitors were taken aboard by water-taxi speedboats operating from the harbor edge. Dancing and a water "thrill" show, the highlight of which was an Acapulco high-diving stunt performed four times daily, captivated her customers while they became familiar with the ship. At a climax of the Shrine Convention there, she was christened by Mrs. Max B. McKee, wife of the owner.

It had been a long time since a new liner had been on the lakes, and her broad list of amenities and passenger comfort

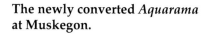

The newly converted *Aquarama* at Muskegon.

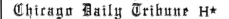

touches would do exactly what the owners had hoped it would do: attract excursionists. She would have all-steel construction with fire-resistant furnishings. To allay fears of those recalling the July 1956 *Andrea Doria-Stockholm* collision on the Atlantic, passengers would be content knowing that the radar on the ship could detect any vessel the size of a rowboat or larger in plenty of time to avoid a collision. She would also have a radio direction finder, an AM and FM radio, and a fathometer. A closed-circuit, four-camera TV system would enable the crew to view the stern and other parts of the ship from the bridge. Automatic fire-closure doors, a twenty-four station smoke detection system, ship-

Looking aft from the sun deck.

Upper deck looking aft to main stage and dance floor.

Main dance floor and club dance floor above.

Sun deck looking forward.

Underneath the canopy on the sun deck looking aft.

to-shore telephones, and four 135-person capacity lifeboats were all incorporated with careful attention to passenger safety.

Perhaps the most well-liked attribute of the liner was the spacious public spaces afforded those who roamed her decks. The large expanses of deck area for gathering, sunning, or lounging offered the traveler plenty of room "to breathe." Brightly colored umbrella tables punctuated these areas to add just the right festive accent. Her two Westinghouse escalators were a hit—the first ever on a Great Lakes ship. The escalators and an elevator would carry passengers from deck to deck with ease. The gleaming corrugated stainless steel siding on each side of the vessel, borrowed from the "new" look on passenger trains, gave her a sparkling appearance. She had wide, push-button, watertight, auto-access doors and a flashing traffic signal control system on her auto decks. Her open-countered ship's office, baggage check, novelty, and cigar shops near the main stairs seemed extra convenient for passengers. A gift shop, novelty games, photo booth, and voice recorder were in the carnival room. A playroom, with a baby-sitting service for children two to six, had a tricycle, blackboard, books, toys, a flashing lighthouse, and a small model of the *Aquarama* complete with a kiddie-operated steering wheel.

There were four restaurants offering entrees from the simple to the elaborate. Among these was the main, cafeteria style, restaurant, which would seat three hundred people. Designed for daytime service only, she would have no state-

105

rooms or sleeping accommodations. There were two TV theaters, seating sixty-six and eighty-six people, which could also be used for conferences or special programs. Adding to passenger enjoyment were two observation lounges, large heat-absorbing tinted-glass windows throughout, two dance floors, both near the raised orchestra platform and shell, and aluminum ceiling fans. Marine motif murals by Pierre Bourdelle added yet another dimension to the sophisticated surroundings. Her bright red, dummy smokestack, which housed quarters for the captain and ship's officers, presented a streamlined appearance similar to the look of the ocean liners of the day. Her real smokestack, smaller in diameter and made of aluminum, incorporated the mainmast and was designed to eliminate the nuisance of smoke and soot on the decks. The lack of wood in furniture and furnishings exhibited the regard for fire safety (about the only wood to be found on the ship was on the dance floors and the tops of service bars). With a crew of 189 (53 operating personnel and 136 in the stewards department) along with all the comforts, conveniences, and attractions that a passenger could want, the *Aquarama* represented "a monstrous floating invitation to a party."

On June 2, 1956, for the first time under her own power, the *Aquarama* departed Muskegon for a weekend shakedown run. Commanded by Capt. Robert Leng, she sailed across Lake Michigan to Milwaukee. She would be under the watchful eye of the Coast Guard, aboard to observe and certify her for full-fledged operation. Also along on this first trip was a large gang of newsmen preparing for a nationally televised broadcast about the St. Lawrence Seaway on "Wide Wide World." Passing her inspection "satisfactorily," she reached a speed of about thirteen miles per hour. For the rest of the season, she would be busy exhibiting her luxuries during several short familiarization cruises at ports in Wisconsin, Muskegon, Buffalo, Detroit, and Cleveland.

Captain Leng, who turned the ship in the eight hundred-foot basin at Racine in July, remarked, "She was as light as a bird." Too light probably, for high winds caused the cancellation of a scheduled July 9 cruise at Cleveland. Scheduled sailings were at 10:00 A.M. to 2:00 P.M., and an evening cruise from 7:00 to 11:30. Fares ranged from $2.50 to $4.75, with children under twelve at half fare. Already some twenty-three thousand passengers, despite her erratic schedule, had crossed her decks. Then, her Detroit arrival, delayed a day because of electrical and mechanical difficulties said to have been incidental to her conversion, disappointed the crowd

So Many Things to SEE...to ENJOY!
You'll Find Adventure and Excitement
on Every Deck!

5 Stairways
6 UPPER DECK
7 Main Lounge Lobby
8 Ship's Office
9 Main Dining Buffet
10 Carnival Room &
    Novelty Shop *
12 Soda & Sandwich Bar
13 Galley
14 Check Room
15 Candy, Cigarette
    & Souvenir Counter
16 Escalator
17 Main Bar
18 Main Dancing
19 Mariner's Bar
20 Lounge Sun Deck
21 CLUB DECK
22 Club Deck Dancing
23 Club, Soda & Sandwich Bar
24 Club Main Lounge
25 Fireplace and Library
26 Children's Playroom & Puppet Theatre
27 Forward Club Lounge

*Down Forward
Stairway in Main
Dining Buffet

Telephones, Exhibits, Tourist Auto Space on ENTRANCE DECK

28 Forward Sun Deck
29 Lounge TV Room
30 Club Theatre Room
31 Circular Stairway
32 SPORTS DECK
33 Club Bar
34 Observation Lounge
35 Forward Observation Deck
36 SUN DECK

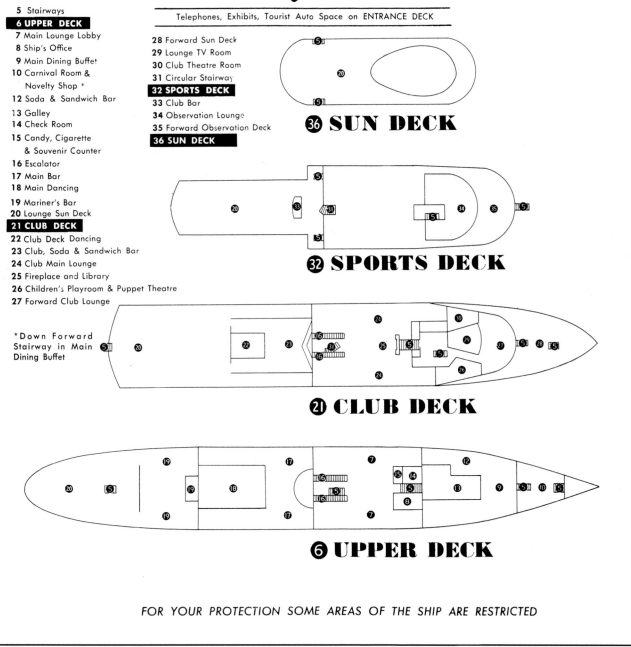

36 SUN DECK

32 SPORTS DECK

21 CLUB DECK

6 UPPER DECK

FOR YOUR PROTECTION SOME AREAS OF THE SHIP ARE RESTRICTED

The *Aquarama* dwarfs automobiles at a Detroit dock, June 1956.

anxiously waiting for the beginning of a series of "get acquainted" cruises into Lake St. Clair and the St. Clair Flats. Those problems were overcome on June 21, after the weather had threatened all day; clear skies presented a perfect sunset to greet some two thousand passengers, many from the Detroit Athletic Club and the Chamber of Commerce. Said to have been a quiet cruise, few seemed to notice that the big ship was in motion. The escalators got their first good workout as they constantly moved people from deck to deck. Most of her guests enjoyed a shrimp dinner followed by an evening of dancing. However, as can happen on a new vessel until everything falls in place and the crew "gets in the groove," everything did not run smoothly. Some passengers were disgruntled at having to stand in line for an hour and a half finally to discover that they couldn't be served. Docking delays made one unhappy Jaycee, Norman Cummings, complain that an estimated fifteen hundred people could hardly wait to get off the vessel and were made to leave through a single exit down a narrow stairway.

Back in Detroit for more short cruises in August 1956, winds on the Detroit River again played havoc with her operations. This time, though, the mishap would be embarrassingly displayed in a large pictorial newspaper story with the headline AQUARAMA MAKES ILLEGAL ENTRY AT WINDSOR. With her propeller turning full speed astern, she dragged both anchors through a tangle of cables in an effort to complete her turn in the current and the thirteen-mile-per-hour,

108

west (upstream) winds. Plowing into and damaging twenty-five feet of seawall, she knocked down ornamental iron railings and embedded her nose in the rubble fill behind the seawall. Workmen planting a garden nearby sprinted to safety. They had heard the loudspeakers on the ship telling them to "get out of the way, we're going to hit." None of the 1,096 aboard were injured. Marine experts declared that her hull and her new superstructure acted like a huge sail, believing that the vessel could not be turned against the wind. Making daily alternate cruises on Lake St. Clair and Lake Erie as part of the Detroit Riverama celebration, she had been turning in the Detroit River to head to Lake Erie. About three feet of her bow was dented and a large amount of paint was scraped away on the port side.

Before the 1957 season, the *Aquarama* was sent to a Chicago shipyard for routine repairs and enlargement of her rudder surface to give her more maneuverability in close quarters. As a saltwater cargo vessel, her rudder only had a control surface aft of the rudderpost, which did not push enough water, it was thought. Therefore, more surface was added forward of the shaft to make the rudder act more like "a door" and possibly assist her in turning. Capt. Morgan L. Howell, who had spent thirty-five years on the Great Lakes, oceans, and rivers of the world, would be the new skipper. Howell had served as executive officer on both the *North* and *South American*, the *Put-in-Bay*, and was also second mate on

"Going on an ocean voyage on the Great Lakes," passengers board at Detroit. (Courtesy Marlene Porter)

The old and the new. The proud *Aquarama* glides by the old D&C liners *Eastern States* and *Greater Detroit.*

the *Aquarama* in 1956. It was hoped that with the rudder alteration and a new captain, the upcoming season would mark the end of her problems, but complications continued to plague the vessel.

At Cleveland she struck a dock and backed into a breakwater as she was turning for her return trip to Detroit. Then there was an incident that angered residents along the St. Clair River. Witnesses said the vessel kicked up huge waves that overturned some boats and dashed others on the shore or against docks. Two men fishing nearby reported that their boat was picked up by a giant wave, carried some seventy-five feet, and deposited on a livery dock. One boat was lifted out of the water to a height of seven feet above the waterline and smashed on the dock, beyond repair. Other boats were lost from a tidal wave that was created after the river water that was sucked from beneath them surged back and sank them. The *Aquarama* had passed downbound at high speed about 2:00 A.M. on June 21. On that same day, the vessel was again jinxed by winds that delayed her departure some ninety minutes.

New wide ramps were finally completed at Cleveland and Detroit to eliminate bottlenecks that caused much criticism the previous year. The owners claimed that the new ramps could load 2,000 passengers and two hundred automobiles in twenty minutes. She still had delays and problems turning because of winds, but these slight misfortunes seemed to be overlooked by the 13,353 passengers who boarded her for fun and frolic during the first two weeks of her 1957 season. It seemed to be all in fun. Sure, people were laughing at her troubles but they still loved her. Not only that, but the continuing rash of problems gave her a lot of publicity, most of which helped in the long run. On Sunday, July 14, three small boats carrying twelve people were swamped by her wake in the lower Detroit River. Federal authorities investigated and the Coast Guard checked her log, which did not document her speed. Captain Howell stated that the ship was "definitely" traveling at a safe rate. He condemned the gathering of small craft in the big shipping channel and said that "small boats are our biggest problem," adding that "a lot of small boat pilots are thrill seekers." She would end the season with her owners "more than happy" with the seemingly revived passenger business. In all, 52,745 passengers and 2,678 autos rode her on the Detroit to Cleveland trips.

In 1958, with Captain Howell again in command of the vessel, the owners decided to cut the time she stayed at her ports from 2 1/2 hours to only 30 minutes. The previous long stay offered passengers a bus sightseeing trip. Assuming that people take a lake cruise to cruise on the lake rather than ride a bus, the management wanted to make the vessel the prime attraction. Coming out of her winter lay-up at the new Cleveland West Third Street pier, the Aquarama began running special cruises out of Buffalo and chartered sailings out of Cleveland, which preceded her official season operations. Regular season round-trip fares were $10.35 for an adult and $5.18 for children under twelve on the Lounge Deck or $13.85 per adult and $6.93 for children on the Club Deck. The excursions, billed as a one-day "ocean voyage," left Cleveland at 9:30 A.M. and arrived at Detroit at 2:50 P.M, then departed Detroit at 3:20 to arrive back in Cleveland at 10:30 P.M. Who wouldn't love to have the opportunity to dance under the stars on such a moonlight excursion today?

The Aquarama brought a new sound to the Great Lakes in 1959. Imported from the Kockums Shipyard in Malmumö, Sweden, a new "Super-Tyfon" air horn was installed on the vessel. Chosen for its carrying power and pleasant tone, it was audible for nine miles in calm weather, while it could hardly be heard by passengers from its position on the radar mast. Ill winds once again hampered the cruise ship as she scraped her bow in mooring operations in June 1959, causing an estimated $30,000 in damages. In what became an almost common expression, a news article out of Cleveland stated

The *Aquarama* at Racine, Wisconsin, with all her lights aglow.

THE AQUARAMA HAS DONE IT AGAIN. With 450 passengers and 50 autos aboard, the liner was backing out of the Cleveland pier for the run to Detroit in July when she "clobbered" the 675-foot cruiser USS *Macon* at dock and participating in Operation Inland Seas. Only minor damage occurred, but it was enough to cause a reporter to title the story "A Modern Battle of Lake Erie." The big liner closed her season with Labor Day cruises, which served about three thousand Ohio passengers. The season ended, but not without mishap as a twenty-one-foot cabin cruiser capsized in her wake. The cruiser sank after apparently being sucked in by the propeller. Two people were rescued by other pleasure boats in the area. The small craft had engine trouble and was anchored as the *Aquarama* headed directly toward it on her course from Detroit. When the ship failed to steer from its course, the occupants of the cruiser dived overboard.

In October the owners announced that the *Aquarama* might start operations from Miami to Havana, Cuba, and Nassau in the winter of 1960 and continue her regular season on the lakes in the summer. A bill in Washington signed by President Eisenhower would permit year-round operations. However, the Fidel Castro-agitated turmoil in that area made the decision to keep the vessel on the Great Lakes an easy one. In 1961 the *Aquarama* began a series of twelve-hour trips up the St. Clair River and into Lake Huron trying to "bring back the old cruises" and fulfill the wishes of excursion passengers. "Minnie cruises" were also heavily promoted and advertised to lure those traveling by auto around Lake Erie

112

to "forget the driving and lounge on a breezy deck filled with beautifully tanned sun worshipers."

Other than for a few profitable bright spots when the vessel would board enough passengers to make ends meet, the *Aquarama* and the idea of renewed excursion travel on the lakes was fast fading away. After a few seasons of unprofitable sailings, the *Aquarama* was thought to be a possible replacement for the aging *Milwaukee Clipper*. She could carry more passengers and cars and could make the seventy-eight-mile cross-lake trip faster than the *Clipper*. This idea evaporated, however, because the *Aquarama* needed more depth than the Milwaukee dock provided and the owners and Milwaukee city officials never could agree on who should pay for the necessary dredging for this private enterprise estimated at $700,000. On the other hand, the owners of the ship were reluctant to pay a requested $32,000 docking fee. So the once proud and gleaming vessel was put in mothballs at Muskegon. Her sailing days were over.

Then, after being laid up for twenty-six years, she was purchased by the North Shore Farming Company of Port Stanley, Ontario, who planned to update and convert her into a floating convention center. It appeared that she would surely be "born again." In July 1988, with her then eighty-four-year-old skipper again in command, she was towed from Muskegon to Sarnia, Ontario, where the refurbishing was to have taken place. Those plans failing, she was towed to Windsor, Ontario, where, as of this writing, she still waits for a happy ending to her long career. The owner of the vessel, James Everatt, president of S.S. Aquarama, is reviewing proposals to update the vessel for use off the Great Lakes, but still is willing to consider all proposals to keep the ship on the Great Lakes. "Physically, the ship is capable, financially, we're not," he said. Many ask how this could be. Many would-be excursion enthusiasts page through books showing pictures of the grand liners in their prime and with a big sigh lament, "If we only had a boat like this to ride again." Yet, when they were around for that enjoyment, the vessels were forced into retirement because of the lack of paying passengers. Who has the magic plan that will bring back excursion boating and still offer a profitable return for the owners?

Docked at Sarnia in 1988, the still proud *Aquarama* awaits a possible new career.

Souvenir casting of the *Aquarama*.

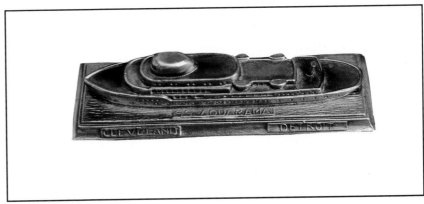

7. THE 1913 STORMS

Soon from his cave the God of Storms
will rise, dashing with foamy waves
the lowering skies.

J. Lamb, *Aratus*

Have we seen hurricanes on the Great Lakes? Most certainly. While the makeup and development of the most severe weather systems that have invaded the Great Lakes are different from that of ocean hurricanes, these monstrous storms are of definite hurricane force and duration with all the ferocious and life-threatening forces included.

Many other deadly and disastrous storms have occurred during the spring and in months other than November, but because the storm that has been called the "worst in the history of the Great Lakes" happened during the eleventh month of 1913, November on the inland seas has become a living legend of the most feared month of navigation on the Great Lakes.

But was it the the worst storm in history? If so, why? First, the 1913 storms produced one of the lowest barometric pressures ever recorded.[13] Not only was this the worst storm on the Great Lakes, according to barometric pressure it was one of the worst storms in the history of the country. Second, a 1988 study by Detroit's WDIV-TV meteorologists, Mal Sillars and Paul Gross, proved that there were two storms—two separate systems—that made up the 1913 disaster. Therefore, from this point on I will refer to the 1913 storm as the 1913 *storms*.

To determine exactly why these 1913 storms are considered the "king of storms," a study of past Great Lakes storm data dating to 1835 was undertaken. A chronological review of old marine weather information and storm aftermath was studied for the number of vessels lost, destroyed, or seriously damaged, along with the number of lives lost in each disaster. Verbatim accounts for most of the storms have been written. This study revealed some startling facts. For simplification, except for a few instances, only November storm data were listed.

November 11, 1835. A storm referred to as a "most terrific gale" hit the Great Lakes from the southwest. This was the first time that a storm was called a "cyclone" on the lakes. It was also the first time that there was a mention of "the wind announcing its approach like the sound of an immense train of cars." This most memorable disaster on the lakes raised "the creek" at Buffalo to twenty feet, floating vessels into main streets and drowning scores of the occupants of harbor dwellings. The loss of life ran into the hundreds; ten schooners were lost and six other vessels were seriously damaged. On the twenty-sixth of that month another gale struck with equally damaging effects.

November 1838. The most severe and disastrous storm in its effects on lake shipping up to this time was experienced. The coastline between Erie and Buffalo was strewn with some twenty-five seriously damaged vessels. Seven schooners were lost along with many lives.

November 18, 1842. A whole gale with winds of fifty-five to seventy-two miles per hour swept the lakes accompanied by snow, which fell to a depth of twelve inches at Buffalo. No storm had ever hit the lakes with a greater violence and destruction to shipping and with a greater loss of lives. There were over fifty wrecks, eighteen of them driven onto the Canadian shore of Lake Erie and many more on Lakes Michigan and Ontario. Over a hundred sailors lost their lives.

November 10-12, 1852. A terrible storm raced across the lakes resulting in the complete or partial loss of fifty-five vessels. Two hundred ninety-six lives were lost on the lakes this season.

November 1860. Because of severe storms, including a terrific gale in November, 578 souls perished in eight months of shipping activity on the lakes. Somewhat eerie was the loss of the schooner *Hurricane* on Lake Michigan with nine lives. To offer some idea as to the volume of lake traffic at the time, a hundred sailing vessels, seventeen propellers, and several steamers passed Detroit within thirty-six-hours.

November 16-17, 1869. The Great Storm of November 1869 entered the record books. This most severe and destructive storm was called the worst in the history of lake navigation. Its violence and widespread gusts swept the entire chain of lakes. Ninety-seven vessels of all descriptions, including fifty schooners, were stranded or foundered during the storm in which thirty-five vessels were total losses. According to the *Detroit Free Press*, there was a loss of many lives.

Because of the countless marine disasters during 1868 and 1869, meteorological observations and telegraph signals between Great Lakes ports began November 1, 1870. This service, credited with saving many lives, had already operated in Europe for several years. The direction of approaching storms, a study of the mechanics of the winds, the recording of atmospheric pressure, and general weather predictions were being practiced with a fair degree of accuracy. Public maps indicating the height of the barometer and the direction and the force of the winds became a useful and appreciated forecasting tool. As for the accuracy of the other tools the early weatherman had, mercury barometers, to forecast the approach of inclement weather, were considered ahead of their time in the late 1600s. Wind speed and direction could be accurately measured in 1734 using hand-held rotary anemometers with dials graduated in meters per second or the Beaufort scale. In 1874 the Lifesaving Service began on the Great Lakes, and though the Weather Bureau had become established, many of its predictions were still based on "old probabilities." When forecasts were not available, sailors could always refer to the appendix of a *Scotts New Coast Pilot Book for the Great Lakes*, which, as late as 1896, contained several pages of weather proverbs such as, "With the rain before the wind, your topsail halyards you must mind." These verses and other weather-related statements were there to advise the mariner. By 1875, storm warnings could be telegraphed to thirty-six stations around the Great Lakes and nearly eighty percent of the storms predicted were verified as forecasted.

November 15-24, 1879. A series of severe storms raged across the lakes, which proved unusually destructive to shipping. Except for one or two ships, sixty-five vessels met with disaster from the heavy weather.

October 16, 1880. A storm that had a great cause to be remembered in lake shipping circles swept over Lake Michigan with winds said to have exceeded 103 miles per hour. Balmy sixty-five-degree temperatures quickly fell to below freezing as southwest gales wrecked or badly damaged ninety vessels and claimed 118 lives of which 75 were lost on the liner *Alpena*.

November 11, 1883. This navigation season was called a disaster; losses were worse than in 1881 and 1882 combined.

Three great storms occurred on the lakes in May, September, and in November, which was the worst. Nearly two hundred lives were lost along with over a hundred vessels that were total losses. The November storm, recorded as having lasted nearly two weeks, sent vessel property damages to $1,150,000.

In 1894 weather bulletins were telegraphed each morning at 10:15 to harbormasters and other principal ports on the Great Lakes. This "extended" forecast was chiefly to predict the force and direction of the winds for the following thirty-six hours.

October 25, November 8 and 18, 1898. Called the most disastrous season in the history of the lakes, total and partial losses amounted to 569 vessels. Three hundred sixty-nine of these losses were directly attributed to three severe storms late in the shipping season.

The first of these, October 25, is reported to have lasted thirty-six hours. According to the Great Lakes Historical Society storm records, ninety-five lives were lost on the lakes this year. However, conflicting statistics are found in the 1899 *Report of the United States Lifesaving Service.* This report states that despite the disastrous tempests that occurred during October and November involving twenty-eight vessels and 162 persons, not one of these perished; and further, that only three persons were lost during the season. What is the reason for the wide difference in the number of lives lost? An organization whose purpose it was to save lives may not have been watching the figures that closely and may have listed only the lives lost where their organization was involved. The completion and maiden voyage of the largest vessel on the lakes, the 476-foot, 50-foot beam, steel propeller *Samuel F. B. Morse,* was also noted this year.

November 27, 1905. Although strong northeast winds were forecast only at Duluth, the worst storm to hit Lake Superior pushed a blizzard of seventy mile-per-hour winds across the lake to sink or destroy five vessels and claim the lives of thirty-seven seamen. A dozen other vessels were badly damaged or driven ashore. This storm is often referred to as the second worst storm on the lakes.

November 7-10, 1913. The hurricane-type storms that hit the Great Lakes at this time took the lives of 235 sailors. Twelve major vessels were lost with all hands; eight of them sank in Lake Huron. The staggering losses included the largest vessel on the Lakes, the *James Carruthers,* a 550-foot vessel only six months old, and two British-built steamers, the *Wexford* and the *Leafield.* Six more vessels were destroyed

and twenty more received serious damage. Winds of at least sixty-two miles per hour lasted for more than nine hours straight. Gusts of seventy-nine miles per hour were clocked at Cleveland where twenty-two inches of snow fell. Eyewitness accounts tell of thirty-five-foot waves on Lake Huron along with a rapid drop in temperature, which was believed to have caused heavy ice to form on the ill-fated vessels.

Even though there are incredible losses that glare out of the documented writings about other Great Lakes storms, the most profound reasons that the 1913 storms stand out above all the others are: (1) at least one vessel was lost—with all hands—on each of the lakes except Lake Ontario; (2) the unbelievable circumstance of the ferocious bombardment of at least sixty-two-mile-per-hour sustained winds lasting for nine hours nonstop; (3) the bizarre incident of the big "mystery ship," *Charles S. Price*, capsizing and remaining upside down and unidentified while word of this strange predicament went around the world. Newspaper and periodical photography, just coming into its own at this time, did much to ignite public interest and help the reader, for the first time, relate to the chilling severity of a disaster *through photography*. The famous photograph of the upside-down *Price* is believed to have been the first time that a photograph was used in conjunction with a major marine disaster. Obversely, in 1898, when more vessels (569) were lost in storms that were nearly as severe as in 1913, none of these vessels had the "mystery ship" attraction nor were they photographed as in 1913. So, even in how the disaster was reported, the 1913 storms were unlike any other previous storm; and (4) uncanny incidents resulting from the storm, the mysteries of which remain unsolved, have made it all the easier to recall the great storms of 1913 as the worst of all.

8AM

8PM

FRI
11/7

SAT
11/8

SUN
11/9

MON
11/10

TUES
11/11

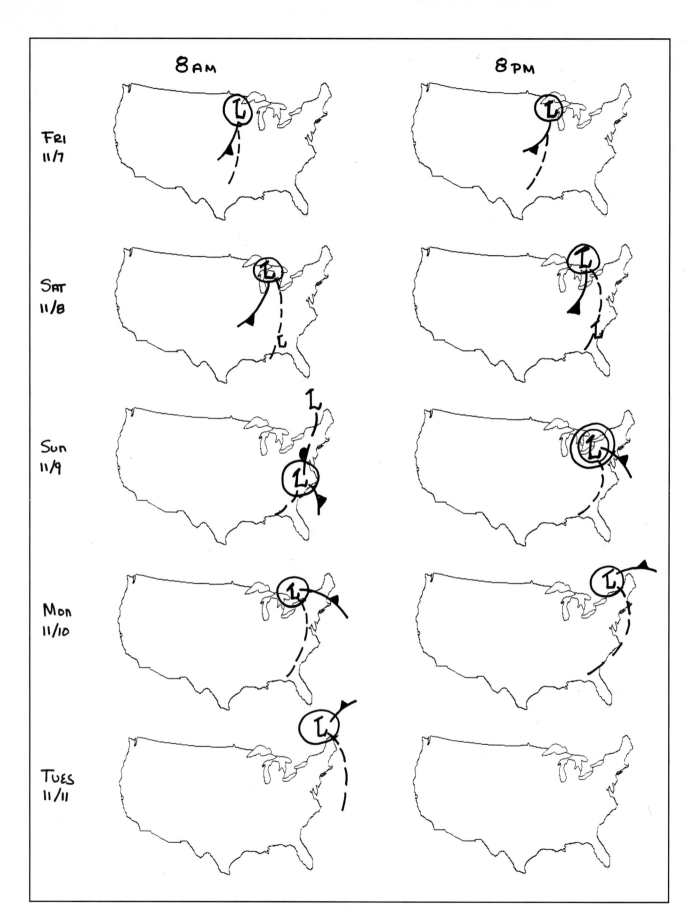

120

ORIGINAL MONTHLY RECORD OF OBSERVATIONS at *Buffalo. N.Y.*, for the Month of NOV 1913, 191

Hourly Wind Velocity.   Maximum Velocity for the hour in red when it exceeds 46 miles per hour.   (Standard of time in local use, 75 meridian.)

Date	0 to 1	1 to 2	2 to 3	3 to 4	4 to 5	5 to 6	6 to 7	7 to 8	8 to 9	9 to 10	10 to 11	11 to 12 Noon	Noon to 1	1 to 2	2 to 3	3 to 4	4 to 5	5 to 6	6 to 7	7 to 8	8 to 9	9 to 10	10 to 11	11 to 12 Mid't.	Total	Max. Vel. (h)	Dir.	Hr. Vel.	Date
										58	55	58	58	57	56	56	54	48	48		48								
1	30	32	32	34	37	38	36	36	37	50	53	53	54	53	49	51	49	45	41	40	43	37	36	32	998	58	W	62-W	1
2	27	23	20	21	18	13	14	15	16	14	15	21	29	31	34	33	33	27	26	25	23	21	20	18	537	36	SW	38-SW	2
3	19	18	17	22	14	18	19	20	18	24	23	23	22	21	23	24	32	36	36	40	41	42	47	40	639	60	SW	62-SW	3
4	32	29	23	21	25	23	23	26	25	21	22	24	26	28	26	22	22	23	22	20	14	13	19	21	550	42	W	46-W	4
5	21	19	18	15	16	16	15	16	15	19	17	18	20	24	28	25	21	18	20	20	20	18	17	16	452	29	SW	30-SW	5
6	14	14	12	10	12	12	12	8	6	7	9	11	9	11	6	5	8	15	18	26	26	28	27	24	330	30	S	31-S	6
7	24	27	29	28	29	28	22	22	21	21	21	20	21	17	13	20	17	17	16	17	21	19	19	16	505	32	S	32-S	7
8	18	21	18	17	25	21	24	21	24	25	25	26	25	22	27	25	23	23	26	27	24	24	21	16	548	33	S	34-S	8
9	11	11	12	11	8	11	15	14	13	19	27	29	32	33	31	23	21	19	14	24	24	31	37	31	501	42	SE	48-SE	9
10	26	28	33	44	53	57	50	59	60	63	65	63	64	72	67	49	54	48	37	35	32	37	37	33	1167	80	SW	84-SW	10
11	30	33	34	33	31	23	34	36	34	34	33	34	32	34	36	35	35	32	35	33	34	33	30	29	797	40	W	40-W	11
12	26	24	19	20	15	12	11	21	28	27	24	23	23	22	21	23	25	27	29	27	27	25	24	21	544	36	SW	36-SW	12
13	19	15	19	22	21	24	26	26	25	26	24	29	32	35	33	34	33	31	28	30	22	18	16	8	597	37	SW	39-SW	13
14	9	9	7	10	11	12	12	14	9	11	13	12	14	17	17	17	14	9	10	12	9	8	7	7	270	19	NW	19-NW	14
15	10	15	10	11	9	10	10	3	2	4	4	3	3	5	8	8	9	9	8	9	9	9	9	8	184	16	NW	17-NW	15
16	7	10	8	8	8	8	11	12	11	11	13	12	12	12	10	10	9	9	6	3	4	4	1	2	201	16	E	16-E	16
17	5	7	7	9	9	14	14	24	22	25	31	40	41	40	39	38	34	35	37	41	45	43	37	35	674	50	SW	52-SW	17
18	33	30	25	25	26	31	28	29	25	30	24	24	22	20	23	24	22	22	20	16	21	19	20	16	577	38	SW	40-SW	18
19	9	8	9	13	14	17	18	26	29	33	29	30	36	38	42	42	41	42	29	35	42	40	43	45	710	48	SW	50-SW	19
20	35	37	32	29	31	29	27	24	14	13	11	10	16	15	14	14	13	13	9	6	2	4	5	4	405	42	W	49-W	20
21	11	12	12	11	10	11	10	11	11	10	15	19	17	12	16	22	23	28	28	32	34	30	28	33	446	36	SW	38-SW	21
22	34	36	35	36	36	24	25	24	22	26	31	30	26	21	17	19	19	26	32	34	32	34	36	45	696	48	SW	50-SW	22
23	43	45	48	54	52	34	30	29	31	25	29	30	28	28	27	24	21	16	17	20	21	19	17	24	707	56	SW	60-SW	23
24	25	28	31	33	28	35	27	33	24	31	35	38	40	43	38	35	36	27	27	24	17	15	17	7	699	50	NW	52-NW	24
25	16	15	14	16	15	16	13	11	10	12	15	19	27	31	33	48	42	40	26	44	52	51	46	47	655	58	SW	60-SW	25
26	44	42	37	36	33	27	22	21	18	15	12	11	9	7	11	15	17	16	17	15	14	18	19	17	493	48	SW	48-SW	26
27	19	19	22	21	21	22	21	21	23	26	25	24	24	18	20	17	17	17	16	18	15	14	12	10	462	32	E	34-E	27
28	6	5	8	4	5	6	9	8	7	10	10	12	9	8	6	7	5	3	7	6	6	5	4		164	15	SW	15-SW	28
29	7	6	9	12	11	14	14	16	16	17	17	20	19	20	20	20	18	19	16	15	13	17	17	14	267	23	E	24-E	29
30	12	10	10	7	13	10	7	10	9	14	14	11	11	11	9	9	9		8	11	13	8	12	12	250	18	S	18-S	30
31																													31
Sums.	622	631	613	628	631	625	596	637	609	663	686	717	746	750	746	739	716	694	653	715	700	685	680	643	16125	(a)	(a)	(a)	Sums.
Means.	20.7	21.0	20.4	20.9	21.0	20.8	19.9	21.2	20.3	22.1	22.9	23.9	24.8	25.0	24.9	24.6	23.9	23.1	21.8	23.8	23.3	22.8	22.7	21.4	537.5	(a)	(a)	(a)	Means.

Prepared by *J.H. Shipman*   * from dial readings.   @ Changed from 38 to 46.   (7) on nov 1. by the Official in charge   Average Hourly Velocity, 22.4

Opposite page, weather maps showing progress of the
1913 storms based on the given weather data at the time.
(Mal Sillars, meteorological consultant)

The first of the two storms, which also became known as "freshwater fury," developed over northwest Wisconsin on Friday morning, November 7, and swept into the Great Lakes in the form of what we know today as an "Alberta Clipper." That evening sixty-two-mile-per-hour sustained winds were clocked at Duluth, leaving freezing temperatures in its wake. By Saturday evening, after the blizzard had raged across Lakes Michigan and Superior, this first storm began to dissipate over Georgian Bay.

In 1913 there was only one twenty-four-hour weather advisory map accomplished by the U.S. Signal Corps. Weather data from this map were telegraphed to various weather stations, which sent out their own regional forecasts. Forecasters and sailors were aware of the first storm but were unaware of a developing surface low along the east coast that was building the giant second storm.

This unawareness obscured the definition of the storms and profoundly contributed to the heavy losses. It follows that many mariners ventured out thinking that the forecast storm was over when, in fact, they were only in a lull between *two* storms, the second of which was to be hurricane strength.

Ideal conditions caused "explosive intensification" of the system when the cold-front low pressure associated with the first storm interacted with the surface low on the east coast. The growing storm, now one giant system, was centered west of Richmond, Virginia, at 7:00 A.M., the 9th. By 7:00 P.M. the storm had dashed across the Appalachians northwestward to a point northwest of Erie, Pennsylvania, where the record barometric pressure of 28.61 inches was recorded.

What a somber and majestic sight it must have been. As a final salute to the sailors that were lost, ten days after the storm, a procession of over a hundred vessels with flags at half mast crept solemnly up the Detroit River. Under gray and sad skies, thousands of spectators lined the shore, their heads bared in respect.

November 11, 1918. Three newly constructed trawlers, the *Sebastopol, Cerisoles,* and *Inkerman,* built for the French navy, departed Fort William, Ontario, November 11, 1918. The *Cerisoles* and *Inkerman* were to keep visual contact with the *Sebastopol,* which carried a pilot. The French sailors were said to have laughed at Great Lakes mariners' tales of the "fury of the lakes." Only the *Sebastopol* survived a raging Lake Superior storm.

November 19, 1929. Although no known losses were recorded during this Lake Erie gale, it is noted here because

The steamer *Truesdale* fights heavy Lake Erie seas on November 19, 1929, not considered one of the worst storms.

of three famous photographs taken during the storm aboard the steamer *Truesdale*. Even though this storm is not considered one of the worst, the photographs clearly show the tremendous forces involved on the lakes with heavy seas unbelievably raging over the vessel amidships.

November 11, 1940. During "the Great Arctic Cyclone" known as the "Armistice Day storm" or the "Black Friday Storm," a barometric pressure of 28.66 inches was recorded at Duluth. Unusual because it sneaked up on its victims, this storm packed winds of seventy-five miles per hour. Lost with all hands were the *William B. Davock* with a crew of thirty-three, the *Anna C. Minch* with twenty-four, and the fishing tugs *Richard H.* with a crew of three and the *Indian* with five. Two crewmen from the *Navadoc* were also lost. The strong gales in the southeast sector of the storm actually reversed the flow of the Calumet River and lowered the Lake Michigan shoreline as it pushed water eastward. The northwest part of the disaster caught and froze to death forty-nine lightly clad duck hunters in Minnesota and Wisconsin and destroyed ninety percent of the Minnesota turkey flocks.

November 16, 1955. The Coast Guard station at Port Huron, Michigan, flew hurricane flags as the wind gusted to sixty-five miles per hour. It was thought to be the first time since 1913 that hurricane flags were flown.

November 18, 1956. Seventy-mile-per-hour winds were clocked at Port Huron, Michigan.

November 18, 1958. The 638-foot *Carl D. Bradley* broke in two and sank near Beaver Island, northern Lake Michigan, with the loss of thirty-three lives. The southwest storm, which produced winds greater than sixty miles per hour, built up thirty-foot seas.

November 29, 1966. Twenty-eight sailors were lost with the 603-foot *Daniel J. Morrell* in a severe Lake Huron storm that packed hurricane winds. Eyewitness reports from skippers who came through the disaster stated that the storm caused the worst continuously heavy seas they had ever seen.

Scientific confirmation that the Great Lakes are a lot rougher than ocean seas came as strain gauges installed on the *Edward L. Ryerson*, which was sailing on Lake Michigan during the same storm that sank the *Daniel J. Morrell*, recorded a stress of twenty-three thousand pounds per square inch—much more than had ever been recorded on any ocean vessel.

November 10, 1975. The ore carrier *Edmund Fitzgerald* was

124

lost with all hands (29) in a storm with seventy-one-mile-per-hour winds on Lake Superior.

Summary of Storm Data

Number of hurricane-type storms: 20; 19 in November, one in October

First storm referred to as cyclone: November 11, 1835

Most lives lost in a single storm: 296, November 10-12, 1852; second worst: 235, November 1913

Most lives lost in a season: 578, eight months in 1860

Most ships sunk with all hands lost in a single storm: November 1913, 12 ships and crews

Most total and partial losses: October and November 1898, 569 ships

Highest constructive dollar losses: $1.15 million, November 11, 1883, 100+ ships

Highest recorded wind: Lake Michigan, 103 MPH, October 16, 1880

Lowest barometric pressure: Erie, Pennsylvania, November 9, 1913, 28.61"

Longest-lasting storm: November 11, 1883, nearly two weeks; second worst, November 1913 storms

Longest-lasting high wind: November 9, 1913, 62 MPH sustained for nine hours

The 1913 Storm—The *Charles S. Price*

8. THE *CHARLES S. PRICE*

Turning turtle out on the lake,
Twenty-eight sailors she would take.
But what ship was it? How could this be?
'Twas the 1913 storms' biggest mystery.

Sister ship of the *Isaac M. Scott*, the 524-foot long, 54-foot beam bulk-carrier *Charles S. Price* was launched Saturday, May 14, 1910, at the American Shipbuilding yard in Lorain, Ohio. Her maiden voyage on June 6 of the same year, as well as the rest of her short, 3-year life, appeared to be unblemished. However, her owners, the Mahoning Steamship Company, evidently looked the other way when they gave the vessel a thirteen-letter handle, naming her after Charles Siverman *Price*, president of the Cambria Steel Company. She would become one of two vessels[14] lost in the storms that had a thirteen-letter name.

On November 9, 1913, the *Charles S. Price*, commanded by Capt. William A. Black, with a crew of twenty-seven, was upbound in Lake Huron with a load of coal for Milwaukee. She was sighted by Capt. A. C. May of the *H. B. Hawgood* just north of Harbor Beach about 11:50 A.M., "making bad weather of it," May later said. Capt. Dan McKay, on a Detroit & Cleveland Navigation steamer, also reported seeing the *Price* turning around and heading for the St. Clair River about noon, ten miles south of Harbor Beach. These are believed to be the last sightings of the *Price* until about 8:30 A.M. on Monday the 10th, when Capt. S. A. Lyons of the steamer *J. H. Sheadle*, as the weather was clearing, passed within a thousand feet of an overturned hull. He recalled seeing what he thought were oil barrels and wreckage floating near the vessel to leeward.

Captain Lyons was having a time of it himself. Earlier that morning, while he was coming about during one of his several turns, he had braced himself on the handles of his steering wheel; however, so fiercely overwhelming was the power of the heavy seas that he was lifted right off his feet to a near-horizontal position while trying to hold the wheel.

To see a ship sink or in an imminent danger of foundering is an incomparable remorseful experience. Knowing that
human lives will undoubtedly be lost, that the victims are, at
that moment, realizing their end is near, brings about a
solemn sadness that touches the deepest feelings of compassion one could have for another. Many World War II sailors,
having witnessed such a catastrophe, described the experience as one of the most lamentable moments of their lives,
knowing they were completely helpless to render aid to their
brothers. So, too, must have been the feelings of those who
came on the unbelievable sight of the big black hull of a ship
bobbing upside down in the Lake Huron storm-tossed seas.

Later, on the 10th, Captain Plough, of the Lakeview
Lifesaving Station north of Port Huron, was scanning the
still turbulent waters of the lake when he spotted a dark
object riding heavily on the waves. It looked like a dismasted
hull. Plough dispatched the tug *Sarnia City* to the site to find
the shocking spectacle of the steel freighter floating upside
down. The stricken vessel was in the middle of the channel
used by all steamers, about eight miles northeast of the
mouth of the St. Clair River. About thirty feet of the ice-covered bow protruded from the rough seas; the rest was submerged at such an angle as to prevent identification or even
offer an estimate of the length of the hull. On Tuesday, a *Port
Huron Times Herald* reporter and a diver boarded the tug

Sport to go out and try to determine the identity of the ship. Although it was all but confirmed that the "mystery ship" was the steamer *Regina*, they could not see the name on the vessel. The captain of the revenue cutter *Morrell*, which had been standing by the hull, informed those on the tug, through a megaphone, that there was little doubt the vessel was the *Regina*. An incident that highly inflamed the feelings of those in the area marine community was the call to duty, and then the absurd release of, the revenue cutter *Morrell*. In what was thought to be an "ostrich like" judgment regarding the disaster situation on lower Lake Huron, orders from Washington directed the *Morrell* to leave the overturned hull and rush to aid the *G. J. Grammer* off Lorain, Ohio. Matters were made worse when it was later discovered that the supposedly stricken vessel was not only in any danger, but was later reported to be in port taking on a cargo of coal. Fortunately, no further catastrophe resulted from this blunder.

Many believed that the *Price* was beaten into the trough of the sea, as so many vessels were. If she took water through her hatches, which would have increased her angle of roll, it might have also caused her cargo to shift. In such a steamer as the *Price*, it was thought, there would be room left in the hold for the shifting of a considerable amount of coal. This, combined with a constant taking in of water, would cause her to roll deeper and deeper until she had passed her natural curve of stability. In this situation, the buoyancy of her submerged tanks could offer the tendency to roll the ship over, rather than assist in righting her. What astounded those

The capsized *Charles Price*. Vessel men found it hard to believe that a vessel loaded with coal could turn turtle. (Courtesy Gene Buel)

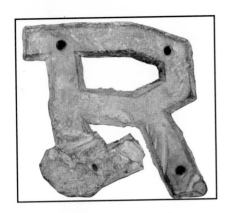

The lead letter R from the stern of the *Charles Price.*

Popped rivets from the *Charles Price.*

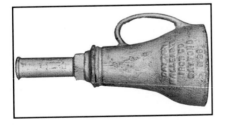

Fuel oil burner from the *Charles Price.*

in the shipping industry was the fact that the ship, loaded with coal, actually capsized.

Those on the Canadian shore found their own chilling examples of the fury of the storm. Seven victims of the *Price* and several from the *Regina* washed ashore together, some of which were reportedly entangled in one another's arms! Other circumstances completely bewildered and shocked those identifying the dead. The body of John Groundwater, the chief engineer of the *Price*, was easily identified by the former assistant engineer of the vessel, which he had left before it departed Lorain. He was asked several times to be positively sure in his identification, for John Groundwater's body had been found wearing a life preserver from the *Regina*. Many other *Price* victims were said to have been found wearing *Regina* life preservers, adding an additional macabre twist.

On Saturday, November 15, William Baker, a diver from Detroit, was finally able to descend along the overturned "mystery" hull in Lake Huron to see the black-on-white letters of the name of the ship and to confirm that it was the *Charles S. Price.* Two days later the forlorn vessel sank after serving eight days as the most grotesque symbol of the storm.

After salvage attempts to raise the *Price* were scrapped, a wreck buoy marked her location until 1922 when it was determined that at least thirty feet of water covered her submerged hulk. Not until 1961 did two Michigan divers, R. Martin and Bill Anson, find the wreck again, about ten miles north of Port Huron. They brought to the surface the eight-inch lead letter *I* to verify their find. Martin found there was a huge gaping hole in the hull. About a hundred feet of the starboard side was crushed inward, leaving a ten-foot gap. "You can see hundreds of rivets that had popped and there are cracks in the hull wide enough to allow a man to go through," Martin said. In later dives, he and his companions retrieved the letters *C, H, A, S, P,* and *R.* William Patterson, a diver from Marysville, Michigan, who was part of Martin's group, made at least thirty dives on the *Price* and was one of the first divers to get inside the forward and after sections of the ship. Patterson retrieved the builder's plate, which is now in the Museum of Arts and History at Port Huron. "Inside the coffinlike surroundings, where no one had been since the ship sank, was one of my most exciting moments in diving," Patterson said.

130

9. THE *REGINA*

Did they pull their brothers from the freezing sea?
Did they help them when they heard their plea?
Could that be why the poor souls washed ashore,
Wearing different life belts than they did before?

Moaning through the trees, a stiff, cold wind lamented a feared warning of a coming storm. Edward Kanaby had just finished his nightly chore of helping his wife with the dishes when I visited his Croswell, Michigan, home, a few miles from the area on Lake Huron where the canal steamer *Regina*[15] had desperately fought the storm that dreaded night over seventy-five years ago. Although the brightness had left his eyes and one almost had to yell for him to hear, ninety-two-year-old Kanaby's recollections of those terror-filled hours on November 9, 1913, during the Great Lakes' worst storm, was still incredibly chilling. Probably the only living survivor of the 1913 Lake Huron storm, Kanaby, then eighteen, was earning $55 a month as a wheelsman on the steamer *H. B. Hawgood*. He described the scene as "a scary, black, spooky-looking sky, with seas like mountains."

About noon on November 9, the *Hawgood*, fighting mountainous seas, upbound and light,[16] was following the 524-foot *Charles Price*, ahead of them about two or three miles, when the skipper of the *Hawgood* announced that they were turning back. Kanaby remembers saying to himself, "Good-bye, *Charles Price*." Soon after they had turned toward the foot of the lake, they engaged a savage snowstorm as the wind increased steadily. Near Port Sanilac, they met the upbound freighters *Regina* and *Isaac Scott*. After passing these upbound vessels, and evidently feeling guilty about his retreat, the skipper ordered the *Hawgood* "hard-a-port," turning again back *up* the lake! That's when Kanaby really got scared, for they found they could only turn back as far as the trough of the sea. Then, pitching and rolling in the deep and menacing valley between the giant waves, they tried to turn the vessel all the way back around to hard star-

The steamer *Hawgood* ashore on Huron Beach, near Sarnia, Ontario.

board. The straining vessel, however, could not mount the immense walls of oncoming water, so the captain ordered an anchor dropped. After this action brought her into the wind, the ship steadied somewhat, so the anchor was raised. Because Kanaby feared for his life, without the captain's knowledge, he gradually wheeled to port, trying to steer his vessel onto the beach. When the captain ordered both anchors dropped, Kanaby breathed a sigh of relief. By 11:00 P.M., the *Hawgood*, dragging both anchors, ultimately came hard aground on the beach of the Canadian shore near Point Edward. Those on the bridge that day were the last to see the *Regina* and live to tell the story.

Many saltwater sailors thought that the vessels built on the lakes that had succumbed to the formidable forces of Great Lakes storms were just poorly constructed. Seamen that had sailed both the lakes and the high seas swore that the lakes were more treacherous, but little did anyone imag-

The *Regina*

ine then that the ferocious storms on the inland seas would later be scientifically proven more powerful than those on any ocean.[17] On the other hand, the mariners who believed that vessels built overseas were of a tougher mold would be shocked at the loss of the Scotish-built *Regina* and the British-built *Wexford* and *Leafield*. The *Regina* had been patterned after lakes plans, but the *Wexford* and *Leafield* were typical British tramp steamers designed to sail anywhere in the world. When present Great Lakes masters have second or even third thoughts about venturing out in bad weather, one can estimate the degree of courage instilled in those who sailed in those primitive vessels one-quarter the length of our modern thousand-footers!

The 249.9' vessel with a 42.6' beam was bult in Scotland.

The *Regina* was named after the capital city of the Canadian province of Saskatchewan. With a 650-horsepower steam engine, the 249.9-foot, single screw vessel was built at the McMillan & Sons shipbuilding yard in Dumbarton, Scotland, and was launched September 3, 1907.

She had two nearly identical sisters, the *Kenora* and *Tagona*, and was typical of the homely little workhorse canalers that ferried cargo through the St. Lawrence River locks and the Welland Canal to Montreal, Toronto, Port Colborne, Windsor, Sombra, Sarnia, and other ports on the way up the lakes. You might say she was a floating general store. Items on her regular cargo manifest might include: oil, steel pipe, tar, spikes, files, baled hay, tar paper, paint, rolled paper, pots and pans, tumblers, horseshoes, fence wire, barbed wire, wagon wheels, ladies hand cream, talcum powder, cologne, skin cream, razors, ladies stockings, medicine, table and silverware, thermometers, canning jars, bottle openers, pails, ladles, stove dampers, matches, cloth, cloth dye, cigars, chocolates, wine, beer, whiskey, champagne, milk, soda pop, lard, salad oil, assorted canned fruit, soup, vegetables, catsup, and English jams. And while her size might sound small, she could carry eight railroad cars of canned goods with plenty of room to spare. Her hull, which had four watertight bulkheads, was lap jointed with half-inch steel plating. She had three cargo ports on each side of her hull along with six deck hatches. Her fore and main-masts were both fitted with large booms used as cranes to hoist cargo. A small wood, five-windowed pilothouse sat atop a round chart room above the Texas cabin on the fore-castle. Pointing the way for her wheelsman during her later years was an unusually placed steering pole, which stuck out of the bottom of her round pilothouse. She carried a crew of about twenty men.

If you ask a meteorologist how bad a storm was, he will

base his answer on barometric pressure. Although the barometric pressure unofficially fell below 28" according to many skippers sailing on Lake Huron during that storm, the official barometric pressure of 26.61" was registered at Erie, Pennsylvania, on November 9. Ocean hurricanes produced lower barometric pressures, but the 1913 storms low pressure resulted in one of the *the worst* ever over land mass.

The first of the two weather systems that made up what is usually but incorrectly referred to as one storm developed over northwest Wisconsin on Friday morning, November 7. By evening, northwest sustained winds at Duluth were clocked at sixty-two miles per hour. On Saturday morning the storm was centered over Michigan as gale winds hammered Lakes Superior and Michigan. A temperature difference of nearly twenty degrees was noted ahead and behind the front. Leaving snow and frigid temperatures in its wake, by evening this first storm was dissipating as it moved east over Georgian Bay. This is when the unusual began to happen. Because there was not an evening weather advisory map, forecasters and sailors were unaware of a developing surface low along the east coast. As the first system was moving out of the Great Lakes on the 8th, this second storm was building along the South Carolina shore. Perfect growth conditions existed as the cold front associated with the Great Lakes low pressure reached the east coast. Interacting with the developing surface low pressure, what is known in meteorology as "explosive intensification" materialized. By 7:00 A.M. the 9th, the growing storm was centered just west of Richmond, Virginia, and winds on the Great Lakes once again began to increase. At 1:00 P.M. the low was positioned north of Washington, D.C. Usually these coastal "northeasters" track up the coast to bring blizzards to the northeast. But this system, because circumstances were ideal for its growth, was accelerating across the Appalachians northwestward. By 7:00 P.M., in a rage of fury it had dashed to northwest of Erie, Pennsylvania, where the record barometric pressure, 28.61", was registered. The storm was at its worst.

Long before dawn on November 9, the *Regina* had taken on her cargo at Sarnia, Ontario. The day before, the mail boat at Detroit posted a special northwest storm warning and both American and Canadian weather stations had displayed warning signals to vessels passing Port Huron. But the first storm of the deadly two-pronged weather phenomenon had passed, and lakemen, thinking that the storm was over, went about their business. By first light, the *Regina* was

Two underwater photos of the *Regina* wreck. (Wayne Brusate)

heading up Lake Huron. With a deck load of sewer pipe[18] and 140 tons of baled hay, she appeared grossly top-heavy. By 10:00 A.M., winds out of the north-northeast began to blow hard and were increasing with a vengeance. Into the teeth of the gale, the *Regina* tried to make her way up the lake. Those on the steamer *Hawgood* sighted her about 1:30 P.M., fifteen miles south of Harbor Beach with seas breaking over her. It was the last time anyone saw her until her wreck was found July 1, 1986, by Wayne Brusate, a diver from Marysville, Michigan.

Ghastly and bizarre reports at the time, along with data generated from Brusate's dive, hint at the terrible chaos that prevailed, but present little concrete evidence as to what took place November 9 on the steamers *Charles Price* and

137

Regina during the worst hours of the storm. What mysterious chain of events transpired between these two vessels held unmercifully in the grasp of this superstorm? The following information is taken from newspaper articles, eyewitness accounts, marine periodicals of the time, and the Brusate dive. It is offered here so that readers might draw their own conclusion about what might have happened on these two ill-fated vessels. True, false, or embellished, the accounts nonetheless present, to a large degree, the absolute horror of the storm.

Highest and steadiest winds occurred on lower Lake Huron between 6:00 P.M. and 10:00 P.M., November 9. Watches on all recovered victims had stopped between 8:00 P.M. and

Underwater photos of the *Regina* wreck. (Wayne Brusate)

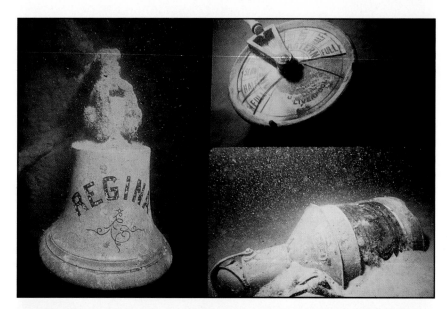

138

1:30 A.M.. Wave heights were reported to have reached thirty-five feet.

About ten miles below Harbor Beach, Capt. Dan McKay, master of a D&C excursion steamer, reportedly saw the *Charles Price* turn and head back toward lower Lake Huron.

The *Charles Price* "turned turtle" about thirteen miles northeast of the Fort Gratiot light. A large deposit of coal on the lake bottom in this area marks the spot of her obvious capsizing.

As evidenced by data from the wreck site, the *Regina* was bowed into the wind on her starboard anchor with her telegraphs at "all stop" and her rudder in the full starboard position. The hands of the pilothouse clock appear to have stopped at either 2:20 or 4:10. Her hull is in the shipping channel pointing almost due north in eighty feet of water, lying upside down off Port Sanilac, Michigan. The *Regina* hull is broken about ninety-five feet from the rudder post. A rupture and many dents in the hull were also found, although the wooden rubbing strakes on the side of the vessel are intact.

About fifteen miles separate the wrecks of the *Charles Price* and the *Regina*. Many believe that this fact eliminates the possibility of the two vessels colliding. However, the *Hawgood* was blown with both anchors down from this area to the Canadian shore near Port Huron, so placing the *Regina* and the *Charles Price* in proximity to each other at sometime during the storm should not be ruled out. The *Regina* was steadfast at anchor; the *Price*, if not colliding with the *Regina*, could have easily been blown very close to her.

People on shore at Lexington, Michigan, reported sighting an anchored vessel the evening of the 9th, which was gone in the morning. There were also reports of people hearing ship whistles.

The body of Herbert Jones, steward on the *Charles Price*, was found still wearing his apron, indicating a hasty exit from his vessel.

Of the eleven bodies in a *Regina* lifeboat that came ashore at Port Frank, seven were identified as crewmen from the *Charles Price* and three were from the *Regina*. The *Regina* victims were from the *Regina* engine room crew, supporting the theory that a *Regina* lifeboat was launched.

Milton Smith, the first engineer of the *Charles Price*, who had left the ship just a few days earlier, identified the body of John Groundwater, the chief engineer of the *Price*.

Spoon from the general store stock that the *Regina* carried.

Wrapped around his body was a *Regina* life preserver. Several other *Price* victims were also reportedly found with *Regina* life preservers.

Looters on the Canadian shore, who were ghoulishly taking cargo and personal effects off victims that had washed ashore, ceased this action and returned some items after being threatened with a three-year prison term. This incident could have confused the reports of finding victims from one vessel wearing life preservers from another vessel.

The captain of the *Regina*, thirty-four-year-old Edward H. McConkey, went down with his ship; his body was found near Port Sanilac a year after the storm.

I believe that the *Charles Price* capsized because of a cargo shift or severe ice buildup or both while trying to turn back toward the foot of the lake. The *Regina's* master, sighting men and the imperiled *Price* foundering in the raging sea, dropped anchor to facilitate a rescue operation. The blizzard conditions that most likely prevailed would have limited visibility to only a few hundred feet. Although fearful of the same dreadful calamity that had struck the *Price*, he desperately acknowledged the pleas for help from the *Price* crewmen awash in the frigid sea. Hanging on for his own life, he hailed word of the coming lifeboat, his screams a mere squeak in the roaring winds.[19] Courageous *Regina* crewmen aft bent to the gargantuan task of launching their lifeboat in seas the height of which they had never seen before. Whatever *Regina* life preservers were handy were quickly thrown in the boat. The *Regina's* lifeboat crew pulled several *Price* crewmen from the sea and threw *Regina* life preservers to others who could not be reached. The *Price*, with her bow grotesquely pitching in the giant gray waves and her stern smashing the lake bottom, became somewhat stationary and eventually sank to her present upside-down position.[20] The *Regina*, dragging her starboard anchor, was blown south and away from the *Price* to her final resting place.

10. THE *JAMES CARRUTHERS*

The brand-new ship came off the ways,
Her life was short, only numbered in days.
The strongest yet built, everyone knew.
But the "King of Storms" would take her too.

On May 22, 1913, undoubtedly the biggest splash ever caused by a newly launched vessel was created at the Collingwood, Ontario, shipbuilding yard. The spectacular side launch of Hull No. 38, the 550-foot, steel bulk carrier, *James Carruthers*, had just taken place. She was then the largest ship ever built[21] under the British flag and the jubilant cheers of those watching the event rightfully proclaimed her the "Canadian Queen of the Lakes."

She was constructed for the St. Lawrence and Chicago Steam Navigation Company of Toronto, and her builders were proud to boast about her many new and shiny features. She had telephones and all the very latest appliances for the safety of her crew. She would have two eight thousand-pound bower anchors, the cables of which were 2-inches in diameter. Each link of her anchor chains weighed thirty-five pounds. She also carried the largest windlass on any Canadian vessel. Except for her deck winches, she was exclusively of British and Canadian construction. She had a cargo capacity of ten thousand gross tons or 375,000 bushels of wheat and had a water ballast capacity of forty-six hundred tons.

Now, it surely takes a while for the bugs to be cleared out of any new vessel, but to have an embarrassing incident take place during her June 11 maiden voyage was never conceived. On the downbound Lake Huron portion of the trip her steering gear went awry and she had to be towed to the Great Lakes Engineering Works at Detroit for repairs. Did any of the crew wonder if this unfortunate event was a harbinger of bad luck for the new ship?

During her third trip of the only shipping season she would see, she was caught in, and victimized by, the tremendous 1913 storms on Lake Huron. Most shocking of all, this brand-new, strong ship, whose paint was barely blemished, was only 172 days old. Loaded with 370,000 bushels of wheat at Fort William, Ontario, and bound for Port Colborne, Ontario, she came through the locks about 8:30 Saturday evening, November 8, and was estimated to have entered Lake Huron around 1:53 A.M., November 9, according to a report by Capt. S. A. Lyons, master of the *J. H. Sheadle*, which was behind the *Carruthers* in the locks. It was probably the last time anyone saw the big vessel.

It is impossible to determine just exactly what agony the crew went through before the demise of their vessel. However, there is more than ample reason to believe that the ship could have iced up to the point where she capsized in

The launch of the *James Carruthers* at Collingwood, Ontario, May 22, 1913. (From the collection of the Collingwood Museum, Collingwood, Ontario)

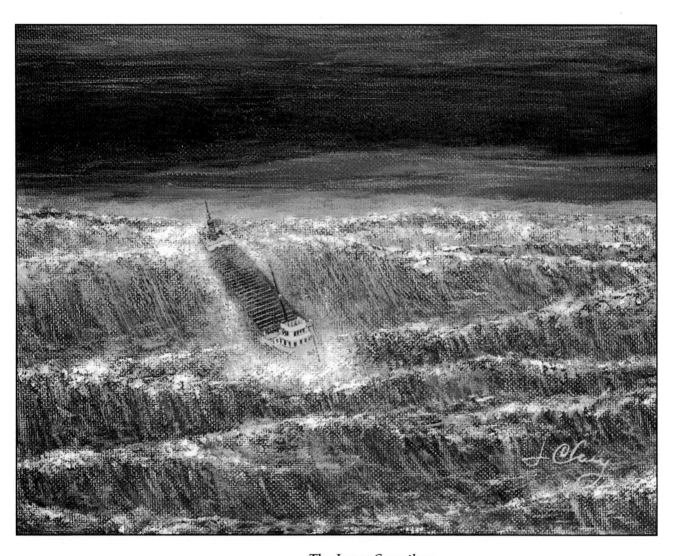

The *James Carruthers*

One of the few photographs of the *Carruthers*. (From the collection of the Collingwood Museum, Collingwood, Ontario.

the heavy seas and fierce winds. Some surviving sailors believed that ice buildup and eventual capsizing was the ultimate fate of all the vessels lost on Lake Huron.[22] In reviewing the destruction of some of the vessels that made it through the storm, it is also possible to conclude that the *Carruthers*, while running before the seas, was assaulted by tremendous following waves that crushed or cleared her aft cabins, causing water to fill and sink her very quickly. Another theory pointed to the possible failure of her hatch covers and consequent flooding of her cargo hold from the tons of water that could have struck her hull. It is also possible that the new vessel again encountered steering problems, which would have, without doubt, made her helpless in the towering seas.

Whatever caused the sinking of the *Carruthers* and other ships that fell victim to the storm may never be fully known. However, all the possible-cause theories and documented destruction of vessels that came through the storm definitely brought about changes in the *Hagarty*, the sister ship of the *Carruthers*, which was under construction at the time. The hatches on the *Hagarty* were changed from twelve-to twenty-four-foot centers, the old wooden hatch covers would be used instead of the newer telescoping design, and the boat deck projection that offered a rooflike cover over the rear after cabin was omitted so that following seas could "roll off" rather than cause so much damage when striking the aft superstructure.

When a boat rudder and some oars from the *Carruthers* came ashore near Goderich, Ontario, November 12, it was the first shocking evidence that this new ship, too, had succumbed to the treacherous storm. Toronto newspapers received a report from Goderich that an empty lifeboat, and other wreckage bearing the name *James Carruthers*, was found on the beach near there. Other newspapers reported

144

that sixteen bodies from the *Carruthers* washed ashore November 13 and 14 near Point Clark.[23] A later report stated that the bodies of eight men and a woman from the *Carruthers* came ashore near Point Clark, November 14. Not only was the loss of the *Carruthers* a heavy heartfelt blow to Collingwood, the city that built the vessel, but it was further deepened because of the loss of hometown crewmen Bob Stone and Joe Simpson.

Defying belief, the most eerie and bizarre incident connected with the 1913 disaster reportedly happened to John Thompson, crewman on the *James Carruthers*. Thompson's sister, from Sarnia, Ontario, certain that her brother was on the *Carruthers*, and on hearing that victims from this ship were being washed ashore, contacted her father, who lived in Hamilton. The father immediately went to Goderich and sadly identified his twenty-eight-year-old son's body. He noted the tattooed initials J. T. on his left arm and the known scar on his right leg. Others also identified the remains after the father returned to Hamilton with the body and began funeral arrangements. As was the custom then, the deceased was placed in a casket and the services were held at home. In the parlor of the Thompson home, where baskets of flowers, family, and friends surrounded this body, the real John Thompson walked in on his own wake! John Thompson, who had been on another vessel, read his own obituary in a Toronto paper. The body that was wrongly identified was shipped back to Goderich.

The *Wexford*

11. THE *WEXFORD*

The salties are stronger, so they said,
Why, Cape Horn sailors come back from the dead!
They can take the high seas, for heaven's sakes,
But they never sailed the November lakes.

High above the long sweeping strip of beach, he steadied himself against the diminishing storm winds. As he gazed down from his favorite scenic vantage point, his breath was taken away at the sight of a body awash in the surf! From where he stood, the clothes the victim wore and the leaden skies overhead made the body appear dark, almost black; but unmistakably, it was a body. Getting closer, he was horrified to see the victim's arms outstretched in a ghastly frozen plea. Robert Turnbull, a Grand Bend, Ontario, farmer, whose property ran along the deserted beach, had just found the first victim of the great storm.While he struggled with the heavy weight, the cold water, and the macabre task of pulling the corpse out of the waves, he noticed that the name "Wexford" was stenciled in black on the poor soul's life jacket. With help from family and neighbors, three more victims were found along with a mangled lifeboat, all definitely from the *Wexford*.

The horrible, long-lasting winds, the blizzard, the unusually heavy crashing surf, and the uglier-than-ever black skies had all foretold landsmen that something dreadful was at hand. Never before had the shore inhabitants from Sarnia north to Tobermory seen the unbelievable sight of the frothing white surface of the lake. Some said it appeared as though the water was boiling. However, not until these first victims of the disaster came ashore did the full scope and severity of the storm become apparent, for word of any vessel losses was not yet known.

Built in 1883 by the William Doxford & Sons Company of Sunderland, England, the 270-foot long, 40-foot beam tramp steamer *Wexford* had the look of an ocean-going vessel. She had flared bows, engines amidships, and cargo booms arrayed on her masts; if she was sighted on the Great Lakes

Victims of the steamer *Wexford* were the first to wash ashore. (Ralph K. Roberts)

today, she would be referred to as a "salty." The fact that she was built off the Great Lakes was cause for a double shock that reverberated throughout the worldwide marine community. Not only did the storms sink a brand-new vessel, the *James Carruthers*, but also sent to the depths the British-built *Wexford* and *Leafield* along with the Scottish-built *Regina*— ships that had supposedly proven their seaworthiness many times over in any weather or sea. Her career already spanning thirty years, she would have the distinction of being one of the oldest vessels lost in the 1913 storms, while having the youngest master of all the ships lost. The *Wexford* skipper was only twenty-six years old.

Having only a twenty-eight hundred-ton capacity, she would make her profits hauling odd cargoes of coal, iron, salt, or freight upbound and returning downbound, usually with grain. On the morning of November 9, loaded with ninety-six thousand bushels of wheat[24] from Fort William, Ontario, the *Wexford* was nearing the end of one of her routine downbound trips. She was sighted by the captain of the steamer *Kaministiqua*, about thirty miles northwest of Goderich, in no apparent danger. By the time the *Wexford* reached the vicinity of Goderich, the weather had evidently deteriorated to the point where Capt. Bruce Cameron felt it too risky to bring his vessel into the harbor. Several townspeople reportedly heard her fog whistles late that afternoon after the blizzard started, and William Ruffell, of the Goderich Elevator and Transit Company, said that he heard what he thought were distress signals coming from the vessel about 3:55 A.M. Monday. Bitter that the Goderich fog signal had not been operating, Capt. W. J. Bassett, the managing

The 270-foot steamer *Wexford.*
(Great Lakes Historical Society)

The *Wexford* at dock in fore-
ground. (Courtesy Gene
Onchulenko)

director for the owners of the *Wexford*, complained at a hearing, "The boat could not have been saved, but if they had known where they were, some of the crew might have saved themselves." Imagine the frustration of the crew members if they did sight the Goderich harbor lights but could not make it in, just barely out of the reach of safety. Because of the constant roaring winds, it is hard to say just how close the *Wexford* was to Goderich harbor. Did she turn her head to the north-northwest winds hoping to ride out the storm or did she try to run before the seas and eventually sink somewhere south of Goderich? Someday she will be found and this mystery will be solved.

Of the seventeen to twenty crew members who were lost on the *Wexford*, Captain Cameron and seven others hailed from Collingwood. One lucky crew member, first mate James McCutcheon, missed the *Wexford* when it left from Sarnia upbound. It was the third time the tardy chap had missed the boat and been saved from an unlucky fate. Not so lucky were the steward and stewardess, George and Grace Wilmott. Planning to return home to England, this would have been their last trip and, indeed, it was. Hospitalized and unable to attend the service, the mother of wheelsman Orrin Gordon could view only her son's casket as his funeral procession passed her window.

The former captain, George Playter, who left the vessel only three weeks before the disaster because of illness, recalled that "it was the craziest storm ever. We never did figure it out and the weather experts were one hundred percent wrong until the storm broke in full force. Skippers got the go ahead from the weather bureau twelve hours before but when the barometer dropped like a stone there was hardly time to hoist storm signals.[25] Hoisting of storm signals was of no use then because ships had cleared from fifty ports from Superior to Goderich and it was too late. I sat at home and watched the barometer. The arrow dropped until it actually bent. I never saw it so low in half a century of sailing and I knew then that the death toll would be high. When I heard the *Wexford* was loaded with steel rails I knew she didn't have a chance. The *Wexford* always gave me trouble when loaded with heavy bulk cargo. She must have sunk in minutes."

In 1975 the wreck of the *Wexford* was believed to have been found just north of Goderich harbor by a team of Canadian divers; but proof of the find was never substantiated.

12. THE *ARGUS*

The engineer gave the lady his coat,
For his being saved was quite remote.
The captain's life preserver she also wore,
For another human, one could do no more.

What kind of meals do you plan for a hungry bunch of sailors when you're expecting the weather to be bad and the ship is already rolling heavily? The regular menu might be suitable, but if the storm became bad enough to wet the galley tables,[26] the men would probably want a light meal rather than something that "stuck to their ribs." These thoughts may have wandered through the mind of Mrs. Walker, the stewardess on the steamer *Argus*, as the vessel entered Lake Huron, upbound from Buffalo with a big cargo of coal for south Chicago. She was, likely, not afraid of the ominous-looking skies and the talk of the approaching storm, but was probably more concerned with how to keep twenty-three other crewmen well fed. Any sailing cook knows that a well-fed sailor is a contented one. Mrs. Walker was, undoubtedly, well liked and respected by the crew. Convincing evidence of this admiration came, however, in a shocking and convincing manner. After the *Argus* fell victim to the storm, the body of Mrs. Walker washed ashore wearing the heavy overcoat of one of the engineers and the life preserver from Capt. Paul Gutch, master of the *Argus*. This offered moving proof of the heroism and bravery that took place during the desperate, dying hours of the ship, especially when the body of the captain came ashore without a life preserver!

Hull number 326, launched at noon, August 5, 1903, as the *Lewis Woodruff*, was a 436-foot long, 50-foot beam, 4,707-ton, bulk carrier built by the American Shipbuilding Company of Lorain, Ohio. The vessel was christened by Miss Martha Wood of Bellevue, Ohio, and named in honor of Capt. Lewis Woodruff, a well-known citizen of Sheffield, Ohio. Evidently not considered an unlucky issue by the owners at the time, giving the ship a name with thirteen let-

The *Argus* was launched as the *Louis Woodruf*—a thirteen-letter name! (Great Lakes Historical Society)

ters would have been seriously regarded as foolhardy and "asking for trouble" in some circles of the shipping industry. Many would say that those old superstitions died long ago with the end of the sailing-ship era. To the contrary, superstition was not only very much alive in 1903, but has also been carried forth into modern times.[27] At any rate, her name was changed to *Argus* when she was acquired by the new Interlake Steamship Company in the spring of 1913. Still, she was christened with that thirteen-letter name.

Loaded with sixty-eight hundred tons of soft coal, the *Argus* passed Port Huron, Michigan, in the early hours of November 9. Had the weather not moderated at that time, Captain Gutch might have elected to anchor in the safety of the St. Clair River. But because the second storm of the two-pronged, giant weather system was not forecast, Gutch, like so many other skippers, ventured into Lake Huron unaware of the catastrophe that awaited him. Some insight into the violent sea conditions and the damages inflicted on many of the vessels that made it through the storm came from reports of the skippers who witnessed the havoc on those ships. Even with these after-the-fact accounts, it is difficult to comprehend what a ship must have looked like out there in the raging fury. Short of a photograph, the only eyewitness account of any vessel lost in the storms was a verbal descrip-

The *Argus*

tion of the *Argus* observed as she was losing the battle for her life at the height of the storm.

Capt. W. C. Iler, while fighting to save his own vessel, the *George C. Crawford*, caught sight of what he believed to be the *Argus* between heavy snow squalls. He later reported, "The storm got her around in the trough of the sea and she appeared to crumple like an eggshell and disappear."

Crewmen on other vessels in the storm told of the near-impossible and lengthy efforts to keep their ships headed into the onslaught of gigantic and rapidly successive seas. This being the situation, one can only imagine what calamity would take place when a vessel would "fall off" in the trough of the sea and expose its full length to the menacing assault of the giant waves. Encountering near-hurricane winds and probable heavy ice buildup, it seems a distinct possibility that the victimized vessels either capsized or had their upper superstructures crushed, causing them to founder.

According to the 1914 *Marine Review*, the cargo of coal on the *Argus* was insured for $15,000, but the vessel itself, valued at $136,000, was not insured, probably because the *Argus* was only ten years old, the owners were willing to cover their own risk by not insuring the vessel. Instead, they relied on a special emergency fund for damages should the vessel be lost, a common practice with many of the larger shipping companies.

The *Argus*, believed to have been sighted as she disappeared. (Great Lakes Historical Society)

Wreckage and bodies from the *Argus* washed in along the seventy-five-mile shoreline from Point Franks to Kincardine, Ontario. A lifeboat also came ashore near Goderich, Ontario, indicating that a boat from the vessel may have been launched. Other wreckage offered proof of the tremendous forces that prevailed as the vessel sank. Capt. E. O. Whitney, an appointed official from the Pickands, Mather Company, the firm that managed the fleet, examined some hatch covers from the *Argus* and the *Hydrus* that were found on the beach near Kincardine. He stated, "They all showed evidence of being torn from their fasteners, indicating that pressure from beneath had forced the hatches off when they foundered."

While searching for the bow section of the *Daniel J. Morrell*, which sank November 29, 1966, Richard T. Race, a Chicago diver, in his underwater search vessel *Neptune*, found a large hulk some 3 miles north of the stern section of the *Morrell*. This wreck was located about eleven miles northeast of Pointe Aux Barques, Michigan. The ship was lying upside down in about 230 feet of water. Near the bow, there was a five- to six-foot cavern underneath the hull; he looked in and saw part of the white, upper superstructure of the vessel. Though not swimming the full length of the ship, Race believed that the hull was in one piece. There were large deposits of coal all around. After completing fifteen of his twenty dives to the wreck, Race caught sight of a bit of white paint showing on the side of the hull. A closer examination revealed the painted-on letters *G* and *U*. During his next dive, September 1, 1973, using a scrub brush, he carefully removed sixty years of surface grime to reveal that the vessel he found was the *Argus*.

The *John A. McGean*

13. THE *JOHN A. MCGEAN*

Who knows what ghastly horrors prevailed,
During the freezing gale in which they sailed.
For they lashed themselves to the pitching craft,
Those three dead sailors on the *McGean* raft.

The launching of a ship is always a special occasion. Just the enormous and spectacular wave created by a vessel as it meets the water is enough to thrill any onlooker. The jubilant and boisterous cheers of builders, townspeople, and special dignitaries who came to see the spectacle would easily drown out the unusual deep rumbling sound a ship makes as it glides down the ways. Often, the screech and blast of factory, boat, and even train whistles add to the fanfare. It is usually a gratifying and happy event, too. Those who spent countless hours constructing the vessel rejoice in knowing that their man-hours resulted in the birth of the ship. The spectators, having little doubt the vessel will float, instinctively shout their hurrahs with unrestrained gusto at the electrifying sight.

The launching of the bulk carrier *John A. McGean*, at noon on Saturday, February 22, 1908, at the American Shipbuilding Yard in Lorain, Ohio, however, was marred by an unfortunate incident. When a mishap occurs at the launching of any vessel, it is considered by many a bad omen, and the ship is, from then on, "marked" as unlucky. The launching party came to Lorain in a special car over the "Lakeshore Electric" and was one of the largest groups to take part in a launching there. Many prominent vesselmen, along with their wives and friends from Cleveland, were present to witness the event. Master John Andrew McGean, the sixteen-year-old lad after whom the ship was named, could not attend the ceremonies because of a sickness in the family. McGean was the son of Walton H. McGean, a co-investor with John Hutchinson, the founder of the Hutchinson Steamship line. When christened by Miss Marie Johnson of Cleveland, the 452-foot long, 52-foot beam, 5,100-ton vessel slid sideways into the water. The tremendous push of water,

caused by the mass of the hull entering the slip, washed into a platform full of spectators at the stern of the ship. Thirty women and several men were thrown into the deep water of the graving dock. Blanche Thomas was seriously injured when hit on the head by a plank, and Henry Wyer was badly hurt. The unexpected calamity made the rescue highly difficult for those in the icy water.

About 2:00 A.M. on November 9, 1913, a little over five years and eight months after her launch, the *McGean* entered Lake Huron upbound for Chicago with a load of coal insured for $17,900. As the *McGean* sailed into the worsening storm that day, one has to wonder what foreboding thoughts crossed the minds of her crewmen, who most certainly knew of the mishap at the launching of their "unlucky ship." Last sighted some distance above Tawas Point, Michigan, at 10:00 A.M. that day, the *McGean*, on what was referred to as the "direct detour course," was followed by the steamer *Isaac M. Scott*. Both vessels, hugging the lee shore, seemed quite safe from the northwest gale, which, even then, had to be increasing in intensity. An hour or so later, it was conjectured, the winds switched to the northeast and the two vessels headed

158

When *John A. McGean* was lost she was only five years and eight months old. (Dossin Great Lakes Museum)

directly into the blow. It was thought that the *McGean*, then on a general northeast course, could have run aground on Nine Fathom Bank, a shoal in the middle of Lake Huron, where the lake was known by fishermen to have only a twenty-one-foot depth. This theory may correlate with the damages sustained by the propeller of the *McGean*, which will be covered later in this chapter.

The *McGean* carried a crew of twenty-three and was commanded by Capt. Chauncey R. "Dancing" Nye of Cleveland, who had sailed the lakes for thirty years. A former pilot on the Detroit fireboat *James Battle*, Nye had been dubbed "Dancing" because of his love of the party life during his stay at many of the port towns into which he sailed.

The *McGean* evidently succumbed to the storm sometime between 10:00 A.M. and midnight on November 9. On Thursday the thirteenth, three desperate sailors, who had lashed themselves to a raft from the stricken ship, came ashore five miles south of Goderich, Ontario. According to the Sarnia newspapers, a watch on one of these victims had stopped at 1:30 A.M. Two of the victims were identified as wheelsmen Thomas Stone and George Smith, both from a Sarnia Indian reservation. The other victim was the watchman, John Olsen. Later that day, many more *McGean* victims washed ashore. The body of the steward, R. A. Harrison, was picked up ten miles out of Goderich by a search party aboard the tug *John Logie*. Another raft, with one *McGean* crewman, also drifted to shore. Mysteriously, one body found at Kintail Beach above Goderich, having washed ashore with other *McGean* victims, wore a life preserver

Three underwater slides of the *McGean* wreck. (David Trotter)

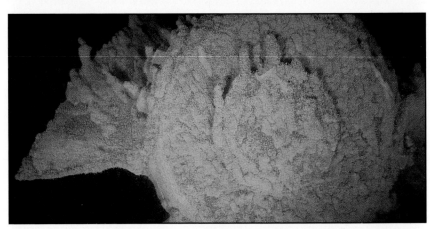

without a name stenciled on it. Known only as "Kintail No. 26," as his was the twenty-sixth body found there, the man was never identified as being from any of the lost vessels. A marker over the grave of this victim, at Maitland Cemetery in Goderich, simply reads "Kintail No. 26."

After the tragedy, as could be expected, people began to question the heavy loss of life and the lack of safe refuge for sailors on Lake Huron. Well-manned and well-attended lights, navigational aids, and foghorns, along with around-the-clock lifesaving crews and a good, protected sanctuary of refuge at Harbor Beach on the American side of the lake, heavily contrasted with facilities on the Canadian side. The largest harbor on the Canadian shore was at Goderich, ironically named the "Harbor of Refuge," but was considered too small to handle the larger vessels then sailing the lakes. With only a volunteer lifesaving crew, lighthouse, and an intermittently operated and alleged inadequate foghorn, the port appeared grossly insufficient in the light of the great disaster. More salt was added to the wounds of hundreds of bereaved family members when stories that originated in the Toronto newspapers contained the headline, NO COMPENSATION FOR LOSS OF SAILORS—AN ACT OF GOD WILL BE DEFENSE OF SHIPOWNERS. The mourning of Captain Nye's widow was particularly painful as she recalled a recent discussion with her husband about their upcoming December wedding anniversary dinner. Poking fun at the possibility of her having dinner without him, he told her to "have a nice anniversary dinner and play I am sitting opposite."

Searching for shipwrecks in any body of water can be a long and frustrating effort. For countless years, divers have been searching the lakes for the remains of wrecks that seem to have virtually sailed into oblivion. Even with sidescan sonar, veteran operators are still baffled in the search for a relatively small target on the enormous oceanlike lake bottoms. Sometimes their inadvertent efforts are rewarded with a lucky find that just happens to lie smack in the middle of their probe.

In 1985, after many fruitless sonar passes, two members of a survey team covering an area ten miles northeast and nine miles off Harbor Beach, Michigan, detected "the biggest wreck" they had ever seen. Several anxious weeks would pass before diver David Trotter descended on the most exciting discovery of his life. He landed on the dark floor of Lake Huron at a depth of 170 feet, near the bow of the unknown hulk. Swimming about forty feet to the cabins, he saw the name on the side of the ship. His heart was pounding as he screamed with joy, for there rested the remains of the John A. *McGean*.

During the subsequent 150 dives to the wreck, Trotter would discover that the giant propeller had one blade missing and another damaged. The rudder shaft was twisted and bent and the rudder itself was situated at a ninety-degree angle to the hull. This supported the theory that the vessel may have struck bottom, damaging her rudder and thereby losing control of her steering. Further investigation revealed that the vessel appeared to have hit the bottom, stern first, and then wrenched sideways, for the hull is twisted to the point where the rear, collapsed cabins are exposed. Trotter believes that the ship may have turned turtle and floated awhile, like the "mystery ship" *Charles Price*.

In limited visibility and near darkness, a diver swimming alongside a hull the size of the *McGean* must feel like the tiniest speck on earth. That is what Trotter experienced during one herculean dive on the wreck when he swam the length of the ship at 170-foot depth. He saw that both anchors were still in place and that the forward mast, stack, and portions of the cabins lay close to the upside-down hull. He placed his hands on the exposed auxiliary steering wheels and momentarily wondered about the tragedy so many years ago. He related that his biggest thrill and most unique diving experience on the *John A. McGean* was his rare opportunity to "literally swim back in time."

It is said that after a big blow you can still find pieces of coal from the *McGean* washing in on the beaches at Port Hope, Michigan. It could also be stated that Captain Nye rests with his ship, nearby, for the "Dancing Captain" was born and raised in Port Hope, just a few miles from the wreck of his ship.

14. THE *HYDRUS*

The *Hydrus* and *Argus*, the *Price* and the *Scott*,
Unlucky sister ships believe it or not.
Related by their particulars, the records show,
And they all were lost in the horrible blow.

Many mariners believe the top "jinx" that could be placed on vessels that have unusually bad luck is the supposed hex attached to sister ships. Changing or altering the name of a vessel, especially in the middle of a shipping season, is also high on the list of things that could bring bad luck to a ship. These beliefs, no doubt, were supported by the loss of many vessels in this category. The original steamers *D. M. Clemson*, *D. G. Kerr*, and *James H. Reed*, all built in 1903, were sister ships owned by the Provident Steamship Company. In November 1908 the *Clemson*, upbound with a cargo of coal for Duluth, disappeared with all hands on Lake Superior. On April 27, 1944, the *Reed* collided with the Canadian freighter *Ashcroft* in the fog off Ashtabula, Ohio, and went down with her crew of twelve. The *Kerr* apparently broke the jinx with a name change, becoming the *Harry R. Jones*. Another two sister ships that were lost were the *Andastee* and the *Choctaw*, built in 1892. The *Andastee* was lost with twenty-five lives on Lake Michigan in the fall of 1929, and the *Choctaw* went down in Lake Huron after colliding with the *Wacondah* in the summer of 1916. The *Monkshaven*, *Theano*, and *Leafield*, three sister ships of the Algoma Central Steamship fleet, would all meet their end near the entrance to Thunder Bay, Lake Superior.[28] Also in the 1913 storms on Lake Huron, two sets of sister ships were lost, the 504-foot *Charles S. Price* and *Isaac M. Scott* and the 416-foot *Hydrus* and *Argus*.

On October 7, 1913, just a month before the big storms, the trim wooden steamer *C. C. Hand*, built in Cleveland in 1890 and owned by the Gilchrist Transportation Company, became stranded on Big Summer Island in Lake Michigan and burned down to the water. The *Hand* was originally called the *R. E. Schuck*, but was renamed when the new steel

The steamer *D. M. Clemson.*
(Great Lakes Historical Society)

The steamer *D. G. Kerr.* (Great
Lakes Historical Society)

The steamer *James H. Reed.*
(Great Lakes Historical Society)

The *Hydrus*

The steamer *Andaste*. (Dossin
Great Lakes Museum)

The steamer *Choctaw*. (Great
Lakes Historical Society)

Schuck was built. Strangely, the two vessels would be lost
within a month of each other.

On Saturday, September 12, 1903, the 436-foot, steel
steamer, *R. E. Schuck* (the former name of the *C. C. Hand*) was
added to the Gilchrist line when Miss Elsie Schmidt of
Sandusky, Ohio, christened the vessel at the launching at the
American Shipbuilding Company of Lorain, Ohio. The
Schuck was sent down the ways just thirty-seven days after

her sister ship, the *Louis Woodruff* (later the *Argus*), was launched. The ship was named after R. E. Schuck, who, it was said, had been interested in the Gilchrist boats for many years. The *Schuck* became the *Hydrus* when acquired by the Interlake Steamship Company in April 1913. *Hydrus*, from the Greek *hudros*, is one of the constellations that make up the Southern Cross.

Like her twin sister, the *Hydrus* had a good but short career lasting just two months short of ten years. Loaded with seven thousand tons of iron ore insured for $28,000, the *Hydrus* departed her Lake Superior port and arrived at the Soo Locks about 8:30 P.M. on November 8, 1913. Having already steamed through increasing gale-force winds that had built great seas in the big lake, Capt. John H. Lowe must have felt that the worst part of his downbound voyage was behind him. His vessel, along with others in the area, was probably showing the signs of having been in a good winter sea. When a ship plunges through big seas in low temperatures, freezing spray can build on the hull to create an unusual, almost mystical, appearance. The beard of ice on the bow and the frozen coating along the sheer of a vessel can look like an expansive, artistic rendering, drawn by the chilled hand of "old man winter" himself. In more serious conditions, heavy ice buildup can add tons of extra, top-heavy weight, offsetting the center of gravity of a ship to substantially increase its chances of capsizing. With this in mind, it is easy to comprehend how such an ice-laden vessel, caught in the trough of giant seas, might easily "turn turtle." Many believe these conditions caused the loss of the vessels on Lake Huron.

The steamer *J. H. Sheadle* also passed through the Soo Locks about 8:30 P.M., Saturday, November 8. Ahead of this

The 436-foot *Hydrus* was under ten years old when she was lost. (Great Lakes Historical Society)

167

vessel was the *James Carruthers*, and behind it was the *Hydrus*. Using the *Sheadle* (which survived the storm) as an example, one can estimate that the *Hydrus* passed out of the St. Marys River and into Lake Huron around 2:00 A.M., November 9. The wind was north-northeast and light. After the *Hydrus* passed Thunder Bay, however, strong winds developed from that same direction; the *Hydrus*, to keep from taking the pounding of the big following seas, most likely shifted her course slightly to avoid running dead before the wind. Off Harbor Beach, a "white-out" blizzard, with estimated seventy-mile-per-hour winds directly out of the north, reduced visibility to near zero. The *Hydrus* was now probably running directly before the gale. Eventually seeing that his vessel could not take the pounding from the following sea, Captain Lowe might have elected to turn the *Hydrus* around and head into the oncoming sea[29] In the trough, between these maneuvers, the vessel, no doubt, fell victim to the unmerciful fury sometime late in the day, November 9. According to the *Marine Review*, the highest winds occurred between 6:00 and 10:00 P.M. that day and

168

watches on victims had all stopped between 8:00 and 11:30 P.M.

Coming ashore farther north than the victims of other vessels, the *Hydrus* victims came ashore near Southampton and Kincardine, Ontario, wearing life preservers from their stricken vessel. A search party also witnessed a *Hydrus* lifeboat come ashore there as well, which bore the grisly remains of five crewmen tightly secured to the seats. One other lifeboat, found later, became a monument to the lost Lake Huron sailors, for it was preserved at Kincardine for many years. When his *Hydrus* shipmates came ashore, above and below him, near the towns of Kincardine and Southampton, Allen McRae, at Inverhuron, realized just how lucky he was, for he had quit his job on the *Hydrus* only days before it sank. The wreck of the *Hydrus*, as of this writing, has not been found.

The *Isaac M. Scott*

15. THE *ISAAC M. SCOTT*

A few bits of wreckage and one of her boats,
No poor souls in their water-soaked coats.
No word for sweethearts or waiting wives,
The *Scott* just vanished with twenty-eight lives.

It was an ideal day for a launching. It was Saturday, June 12, 1909, and the shipbuilding town of Lorain, Ohio, was alive with hundreds of anxious spectators who had come to see the event. According to the *Lorain Times Herald*, "a bevy of pretty girls ever to grace a launching stand served as sponsors" to help send the 524-foot bulk carrier, *Isaac M. Scott*, down the ways. "Seldom were there so much femininity and local guests at a launching party." Exactly at noon, Miss Mildred Noxon of Lorain made a pretty picture as the bottle of wine was broken across the bow of the freighter. Immediately after the launch, the sponsors and special guests were banqueted in the dining rooms of the American Shipbuilding Company.

A ship having such a perfect launch on a perfect day without any unfortunate or embarrassing incidents taking place is supposed to predict that the vessel will have a long and unblemished career. Not so with the new *Isaac Scott*. Her builders and the officials at the Virginia Steamship Company, owners of the *Scott*, surely must have been scratching their heads and wondering what they did wrong. Before she was even a month old, the brand-new ship, on her maiden voyage no less, rammed head-on into the fully loaded ore carrier, *John B. Cowle*. A "pea-soup" fog in Whitefish Bay, Lake Superior, during the early hours of July 10, 1909, with many vessels nearby, all blowing fog signals, set the stage for the collision. The *Cowle* was downbound from Two Harbors, Minnesota. In a very thick fog, how close would a vessel have to be before it could be seen? Too close, in this case. Before the helmsman of either vessel could even think of responding, it was too late. The *Cowle* sank immediately with fifteen of the crew; the *Scott*, drifting a bit after the impact, was soon able to pick up survivors, who were cling-

"A bevy of pretty girls" helped launch the *Isaac M. Scott*. (Great Lakes Historical Society)

ing to wooden hatch covers from the *Cowle*. A tragedy on top of a tragedy occurred when Fred Brown, who had been a passenger on the *Cowle*, was rescued by the *Scott*. He then insisted on going along in a yawl to help a search party look for other survivors. Sadly, his noble gesture ended in horror when he fell overboard and was lost with the others.

Including downtime for her collision repairs and regular off-season lay-up, the "sturdy" *Scott*, sister ship of the *Charles S. Price*, had a short life of only four years and five months, which would be brought to an abrupt end during her encounter with the storms on Lake Huron.

With a cargo of coal for Milwaukee, master of the *Scott*, Capt. Archie McArthur of Owen Sound, Ontario, and his crew of twenty-seven were heading upbound in Lake Huron on Sunday, November 9. Ahead of him was the 550-foot steamer *H. B. Hawgood*, upbound and light, hardly making headway in what was only the beginning of the big blow.

172

Capt. A. C. May of Port Huron, Michigan, master of the *Hawgood*, peering through his glasses saw the *Charles Price* steaming upbound at 11:50 A.M., "She was heading into it and was certainly burying herself. She was making bad weather, but was flying no distress signals. It was just beginning to blow hard at that time." Seeing that it was impossible to go any farther, Captain May decided to turn his vessel back down the lake and make a run for the St. Clair River; he was about forty-five minutes north of Harbor Beach. The *Regina*, also heading upbound, "with seas breaking over her, but still heading into the storm steadily," was passed at 1:00 P.M., fifteen miles south of Harbor Beach. After passing the next upbound vessel, the *Northern Queen*, Captain May related, "The seas had increased to such an extent that we couldn't see her half the time." About 3:30 P.M., May sighted the *Isaac Scott* heading into the storm five or six miles north of Fort Gratiot Light. "I thought to myself her captain was certainly a fool to leave the [St. Clair] River. The wind and the sea kept increasing and the snow got thicker. We couldn't tell how hard it was blowing, but I should judge it was about seventy-five miles an hour from the north, north-east. After while, it got so thick, we couldn't see the smokestack." Captain May and Edward Kanaby are believed to have been the last persons to see the *Charles Price*, *Regina*, and the *Isaac Scott* before they were lost.

Lake Huron, by not giving up any of the victims of the *Isaac Scott*, accomplished what Lake Superior is known for. Not a single crewman from the vessel was ever found. A *Scott* lifeboat, with the canvas top still securely fastened down, and small pieces of wreckage were found twenty-three miles north of Chantrey Island lighthouse, off Southampton, Ontario. Was the lifeboat of the *Scott* torn off the vessel when it sank without any warning to her trapped crewmen? Because it was believed, and hoped, that these items could have come off the vessel without it sinking, families and sweethearts of those on the *Isaac Scott* were going through an especially trying period. There just was not any concrete evidence that the vessel had sunk. Making matters worse, a week after the storm, newspapers that offered long lists of the lost vessels and their known dead also offered extra hope with stories headlined, SCOTT IN GOOD TRIM, OWNERS HOPEFUL. For some, the waiting ended only with their passing. The *Scott* had vanished almost without a trace.

In 1976, sixty-three years after her loss, some of her secrets were finally revealed. Four Milwaukee divers headed by G. Kent Bellrichard stumbled on the *Scott* while looking

At the time of her loss, the *Isaac M. Scott* was only four years and five months old. (Great Lakes Historical Society)

for another ship six miles east of Thunder Bay Island, off Alpena, Michigan. Noticing first the word "Duluth," and then the letters "OTT" on the stern, positive identification of the long-lost victim of the storm had finally been made. Partly buried in the mud, and lying upside down in about 180 feet of water, the hull appeared to be in perfect condition. Bellrichard stated, "She evidently hit the bottom, stern first, and rolled over. Her rudder was ripped loose from the bottom." This might offer the clue, as did the damaged rudder on the *John McGean*, that the *Scott* may have lost her steering and foundered in the troughs of giant seas. Making ten dives to the wreck, the team noticed no big coal spillage in the area and that the anchors still hung in place on the bow, offering further indication of the possible quick sinking of the *Isaac M. Scott*.

16. THE *H. B. SMITH*

Superior, they say, never gives up her dead.
Maybe she'll offer some wreckage instead.
She has no compassion, the legend is renowned.
So, consider it lucky when a body is found.

She was one of five vessels lost in the 1913 storms that were built and sent down the ways by the American Shipbuilding Company in Lorain, Ohio. Launched Wednesday, February 28, 1906, the 545-foot long, 55-foot beam, 6,631-ton, steel freighter *H. B. Smith* was owned by the Acme Transit Company and managed by Hawgood & Company of Cleveland. It was named after Henry Bloomfield Smith, a prestigious businessman, who, among other achievements, founded the National Bicycle Company in Bay City, Michigan, which was later sold to the General Motors Corporation in 1916. She had thirty-two hatches and could carry as much as ninety-five hundred tons of iron ore. Another relatively new ship, she was only seven years and eight months old at the time of her loss. The vessel was valued at $350,000, and was insured, including her cargo, for $376,200.

The great storms would sink at least one vessel with all hands on each of the lakes except Lake Ontario. Big Lake Superior would claim two vessels. One of these, the bulk carrier *H. B. Smith*, was believed by many in the shipping industry to be one of the staunchest vessels on the lakes. Even though the *James Carruthers*, lost in the same storm, was a newer and larger vessel, the marine community was shocked and bewildered at the loss of the stout ship.

In 1913, as late fall was edging closer to winter, it appeared, as it does in most years, that shipping on the Great Lakes was winding down. But as the most dreaded month of navigation approached, shipping companies were gearing up and pushing their vessels and crews to deliver as much cargo as could be transported before the season ended. Heavy demands and constant pressure to deliver the most tonnage on time was an around-the-clock objective for most

175

shipmasters. Far above the normal drive and rivalry to "get there first" was the dead-serious endeavor to "make hay" for the company. Time was money, and money was time, and no ship made money lingering at the dock. Even with these pressing duties, the skippers of many vessels, it seemed, were wary of November gales, but only for a few years after a big storm. Soon thereafter, storm fears and caution apparently gave way to the more urgent, end-of-the-year rush. After all, there hadn't been a major blow since the famous Lake Superior storm in 1905. Besides, it was foolishly thought that recently constructed vessels, such as the *H. B. Smith*, were built much stronger than those vessels previously lost. As if not yet convinced of the documented might of November storms, the same foolish lack of caution is still evident today in this era of superships.

Racing the clock, James Owen, master of the *H. B. Smith*, and a thirty-year veteran on the lakes, was running late it was said, as he had been most of the season. The *Smith* passed through the Soo upbound at 2:30 A.M. on November 7, and arrived at Marquette already behind schedule because of the increasing gale winds. Once in the loading dock, the low temperature was causing the ore to freeze in chunks, presenting a further delay. The heavy winds also hampered the process. Capt. Charles Fox, on the steamer *Choctaw*, remarked, "The *Smith* was loaded on the north side of No. 5 dock. It was necessary to put out his lake line to hold the boat to the dock while loading." While other vessels were out on the lakes fighting for their lives, Captain Owen was impatiently waiting out his loading delays, which held him

The *H. B. Smith*

there until the late afternoon of the ninth. Finally, although the winds were still in the thirties, the storm appeared to be letting up, and Owen, feeling that he couldn't be detained any longer, cleared the loading dock and headed out past the breakwater about 5:00 P.M. It was said that Captain Owen had joked about the storm; but in his hurried departure, those watching could hardly believe what they were seeing. The ship was steaming out into the teeth of the gale, but deckhands on the *Smith* were just then battening down the hatches—not an easy chore even in calm weather. Each of the thirty-two heavy wooden hatch covers had to be set in place, secured, and tarped to be effective against the onslaught of big seas.

Evidently amazed to see the vessel depart in a storm that was still a threat, people watching from shore saw the *Smith* head down the lake, then change course to the north twenty minutes later. Shortly thereafter, she was seen rolling heavily while appearing to be trying to turn around. Captain Fox, on the *Choctaw*, was called by his mate at 5:50 P.M. to witness the unbelievable sight. He said, "I do not think I ever saw a vessel roll heavier." Fighting to get her head into the wind, a heavy snowstorm closed in and hid her from view. One of those watching her fade from sight was lifesaving Capt. Henry Cleary, who remarked, "Captain Owen will soon be back." The storm, at first thought to be blown out, raged on that night and into Monday. Some, on vessels that survived

After the launch of the *H. B. Smith*. (Great Lakes Historical Society)

The 545-foot bulk carrier *H. B. Smith.*

the storm, believed the gusts reached seventy miles per hour on the lake.

There wasn't any definite fear for the loss of the *Smith* until November 13, when she was overdue at the Soo. Already worried on hearing that the vessel departed Marquette in the storm, the owners sent out messages to various ports questioning her whereabouts. She had not shown up anywhere. The *Henry B. Smith* had vanished with twenty-three lives.

After arriving in port on the eleventh, a crewman on the steamer *Frontenac*, eleven miles south of Marquette, reported seeing a floating body wearing a life belt. Because of rough seas, they could not retrieve the body. Then on the twelfth, several oars, one marked *Henry B. Smith*, were found on the beach east of Marquette between Chocolay and Shot Point. Closer to Shot Point, the shore was strewn with bits of wreckage including pieces of white, deckhouse wood. On the beach for several days, it was estimated that the items came ashore sometime on Monday the tenth. The location where the floating body was seen would have been immediately offshore from this wreckage. Many other items definitely from the *Smith* soon washed ashore: another oar, a ladderway, cabin doors, running-light screens, bed pillows, cushions, and unused life belts. The wide array of debris was scattered east as far as Beaver Lake, some sixteen miles east of Munising. More wreckage was discovered on Grand Island. From the condition of the flotsam, it was easy to see that the upper structure of the stout vessel had been crushed to bits. On Sunday, the twenty-first, the body of the second cook from the *Smith* was picked up about fifty miles west of Whitefish Point, and brought into Portage Lake by the steamer *Saxonia*. In May 1914 the badly decomposed body of the third engineer from the *Smith* was found by two Indians on Michipicoten Island. His remains were identified by some papers in his pocket and an engraved watch. Imagine how the second mate of the *Smith*, John Burke, must have felt on hearing the dreadful news of the incoming wreckage and the loss of his ship. Burke, stricken with pneumonia, left the ship in Marquette.

The mystery surrounding the loss of the *Smith*, and when it foundered, was complicated by the strange note in a bottle found in June 1914, at Mamaimse Point[30] on the eastern Ontario shore thirty-five miles from Whitefish Point. The note, dated November 12, read: "Dear Sir: Steamer *H. B. Smith* broke in two at the number five hatch. We are not able to save her. [line missing] Had one hard time on Superior. Went down 12 miles east of Marquette. Please give this to owners." The signature on the note was not clear enough to read. It is hard to believe that anyone on a vessel that had broken in two would begin a message with "Dear Sir." Supposedly under desperate conditions at the time, the note appears to be rather calmly written. Because the *Smith* left Marquette on November 9, and was thought to be lost that night or on the tenth, the note, heinous hoax or real, by whomever wrote it, was believed to be a fake by the owners of the *Smith*. Some vesselmen were quick to comment that because of the large number of hatches (thirty-two) on the *Smith*, she had a weak upper deck that caused the steamer to break in two. Others believed that the vessel lost numerous hatch covers, flooded, and sank with her trapped crew. It was generally thought that the two bodies found were washed overboard, and that the vessel sank northwest of Marquette, for this location would correlate with the wreckage found east of that city.

Regardless of why or when she sank, the obvious bold departure of the vessel commanded by the veteran sailor, Capt. James Owen, will long be remembered as a reckless and outright dare to the ruthless fury of Lake Superior. The wreck of the *H. B. Smith*, as of this writing, has not been found.

17. THE *LEAFIELD*

The *Leafield* and two sisters lost near Thunder Bay
Is one strange mystery, even to this day.
They all carried rails; they all were stout.
Just how it could be was never figured out.

It was an unbelievable coincidence. Were they really jinxed? How could the three sister ships meet their end in the same area, each on a routine trip, all hauling the same cargo? In 1900 the Algoma Steel Corporation purchased the saltwater "trampers" *Monkshaven*, *Theano*, *Paliki*,[31] and *Leafield* to haul iron ore to their Canadian Soo mill and the Canada Iron Corporation works at Midland, Ontario. Alternate cargoes consisted of coal from Toledo to the Soo and grain from Fort William to Midland. On their return upbound trips the former oceangoing vessels would often carry steel railroad rails. Three of these vessels would wind up on the rocks off the small islands adjacent to the entrance of Thunder Bay, Ontario, in Lake Superior. The *Monkshaven*, with a load of rails, went on the rocks off Pie Island in the 1905 November storm. After a freezing night, her crew was rescued. In sad shape after spending the winter there on the rocks, she was finally refloated in August 1906. Then on October 18 of the same year, she broke away from her moorings and went aground on Angus Island where she would eventually break up and remain. On November 17, 1906, in a howling gale, the *Theano*, also carrying rails, lost her steering and struck a reef off Trowbridge Island four miles east of Thunder Cape. Pounded to death on the rocks, the ship sank after her boiler exploded. The *Leafield*, also with a cargo of rails, would follow suit and meet her end on the rocks off Angus Island.

The 269-foot long, 35-foot beam *Leafield* was built by the Strand Slipway Company in Sunderland, England, in 1892. With a well deck[32] and cargo crane booms fitted to her masts, she looked much like the steamer *Wexford* lost in the 1913 Lake Huron storms. As if hinting she intended to follow her sisters someday, on August 17, 1912, she went

181

The *Monkshaven* was lost off Pie Island, near Thunder Bay, Ontario, November 1905. (Dossin Great Lakes Museum)

aground on Beausoliel Island in Georgian Bay, tore up her bottom, and sank. After a costly salvage operation and repair, she was back in service for the 1913 season with a new life and a new skipper. Certainly cognizant of the loss of the other sister ships and the serious grounding of his ship the previous summer, it is hard to comprehend why the captain of the *Leafield* would tempt fate with an already jinxed ship by leaving port on a Friday with storm signals flying. But there was work to do, a tonnage quota to meet, and possibly an impression to make on his new employer, who may have demanded he depart then. Regardless, the *Leafield* sailed for Fort William, Ontario, on Friday, November 7, 1913, at 8:30 A.M. In command was thirty-seven-year-old Capt. Charles Baker with the regular crew of seventeen, sixteen of whom hailed from Collingwood, Ontario. She sailed into the building storm and, no doubt, fought the fury all the way. Rounding Isle Royale, she would soon be within reach of the safety of Thunder Bay.

But it was not to be, for the staunch vessel would take to the rocks off Angus Island,[33] where the remains of her sister *Monkshaven*[34] were still visible. Capt. W. C. Jordan, and others on the Algoma Central steamer *Franz*, reported seeing the *Leafield* for a short time, between the blowing snow, some

182

The *Leafield*

The *Theano* was lost off
Trowbridge Island November 17,
1906. (Dossin Great Lakes
Museum)

The *Leafield* left port on a
Friday and was lost off Angus
Island. (Great Lakes Historical
Society)

The 269-foot *Leafield* was built in England in 1892.

miles ahead of him. Jordan was the brother-in-law of the second mate on the *Leafield*. Then, on November 9, Capt. R. D. Foote, of the Northern Navigation Company steamer *Hamonic*, on the way into Port Arthur, reported what he believed to be the *Leafield* sitting precariously on the rocks near a high bluff of the island, where the water offshore is charted nine hundred feet deep. A tug was quickly dispatched to search the area, but no sign of the ship was sighted. Canadian officials sent out the tug *Arbutus*, which combed the waters off Angus Island, Pie Island, Thunder Cape, and Isle Royale. They found nothing except part of a damaged upper mast, later examined by the former skipper of the *Leafield*, who determined beyond a doubt that it was not part of the *Leafield*. Searching Keweenaw Point and the south shore of Superior, tugs out of Houghton, Michigan, also searched for some sign of the vessel without success. Many thought that the vessel sank after the crashing surf released her from whatever slight hold the rocks had on her.

The shipbuilding city of Collingwood, Ontario, losing twenty-seven sailors to the storms, was the hardest hit of any Great Lakes community. Sixteen victims were lost on the *Leafield*, eight were lost on the *Wexford*, two on the *Carruthers*, and one on the *Regina*. Of the twenty-seven, only five bodies were ever recovered. Virtually the whole city shut down as factories, schools, and stores closed to offer their respect to their lost sons at a mass funeral. As of this writing, the wreck of the *Leafield* has not been found.

Lightship No. 82

18. *LIGHTSHIP NO. 82*

Without permission to leave their place,
The ship was lost except for a trace.
They fought the storm as best could be.
And they gave their lives so others could see.

Of the vessels lost during the 1913 storms, this is the story of the most gallant ship with the most courageous crew of them all. Without question, the vessels that encountered the tempest fought for their lives, but they fought to reach a destination, away from the clutches of the storm. Some made it, others did not. *Lightship No. 82*, however, had nowhere to go! Under the jurisdiction of the United States Lighthouse Service, the lightship was bound by duty to remain on station, in harms way, to guide other mariners to safety, instead of running for safety herself. She would be the second lightship to sink on station.[35]

When *Lightship No. 82* was built in 1912, at Muskegon, Michigan, it was believed that the stout ship could withstand the most ferocious seas the Great Lakes could dish out. The rounded whaleback covering over her forecastle deck was an idea borrowed from Alexander McDougall's whaleback, or pigboat, design.[36] It would offer her, it was thought, protection from heavy waves washing over her bow. The most forward part of this rounded covering blended perfectly with the gentle, sweeping curves of her hull to form the high point of her prow. These graceful lines made her nose "stick up" higher in the air than her deck, giving the small, bright red ship an unusually proud appearance. Her steel hull measured ninety-five feet long, with a twenty-one-foot beam and a ten-foot depth.

Her contract price being $42,910, she was constructed for about $452 a foot. A ninety-horsepower steam engine turned a five-foot cast iron propeller. A steadying sail was carried on the smaller jigger mast aft. By way of conveniences, she would carry a steam anchor windlass and sanitary plumbing and draining systems. Although her primary duty was to "give" light the vessel itself did not have an electric light sys-

187

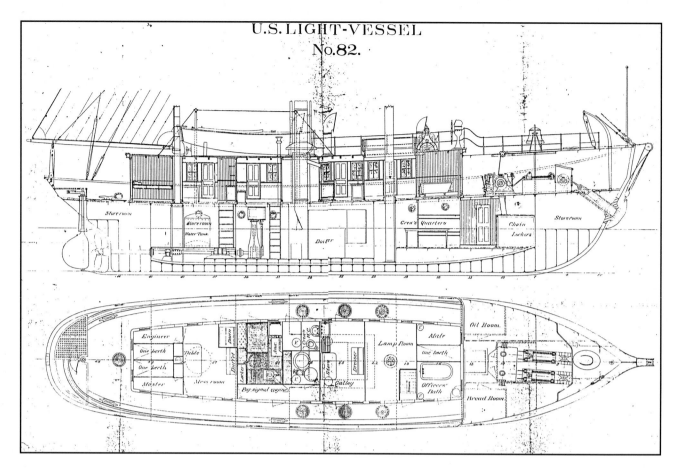

U.S. LIGHT-VESSEL
No.82.

tem. Finishing touches of leather upholstered oak chairs, French plate glass mirrors, and a small library would offer some of the comforts of home during the long hours of duty that lay ahead. Her crew consisted of four officers and two crewmen. The main deckhouse included the officers quarters, mess hall, galley, and head. The crew slept forward on the lower deck. Her illuminating apparatus consisted of a cluster of three 200-mm oil lens lanterns, positioned on a sleeve 120 degrees apart. Each lamp was rated at 170 candlepower. The sleeve, with the lanterns affixed to it, would be hoisted about thirty feet to her main masthead by hand. For servicing or when the lanterns were not in use, they could be lowered through the roof of the lamp room, which was at the base of the main mast. The day mark, a black, oval meshed screen, was also carried on the mainmast above the lanterns. Other navigational fog signal aids included a large bell on the foredeck, a six-inch steam whistle on the stack, a submarine bell, and a hand-operated bell.

Even though the eastern Lake Erie waterways around the Niagara River and Buffalo harbor were considered some of the busiest on the Great Lakes, it wasn't until August 3, 1912, when *Lightship No. 82* was sent there, that a lightship station

for the area was established. The station was first considered about 1903, but did not become a reality until ten years later. Even then, her assignment, "temporarily to mark approaches to Buffalo pending construction of *LV96*," appeared indefinite. She would take position thirteen miles west of Buffalo, off Point Abino, Canada, to guide mariners away from the shallows along the Canadian coast. She would also guide traffic away from the wreck of the steamer *W. C. Richardson*, another hazard to shipping in that area.

Her location was only seventy-five miles from Erie, Pennsylvania, where the record low barometric pressure of the storms was officially registered on the evening of November 9, 1913. Strange as it was, eight vessels would be lost on Lake Huron, which was twice as far away from Erie or the center of the storm! This offers an indication of how very large the weather system was.

That the lightship's beacon was last seen at 4:45 A.M. Monday morning, November 10, is in direct correlation to the height and track of the giant, slow-moving storm. Detroit meteorologist Mal Sillars of WDIV-TV studied the storms and states, "During the night, the storm continued on the move. It was starting to weaken, though, and by Monday morning was near St. Catherines, Ontario, and moving to the northeast. Winds along the Lake Huron shoreline had lessened a bit, but were still in the thirties; Buffalo, however, was reporting winds of sixty miles per hour." Drawing a line from Erie, Pennsylvania, to St. Catherines, Ontario, indicating the track of the deadly storm, it is chilling to realize that sometime in the early morning hours of November 10, as it moved across the waters of eastern Lake Erie, *Lightship No. 82* would have only been a few miles away from the eye of the storm! Most assuredly, had there been other vessels in this area then, no doubt they too would have been lost.

During my study of this subject, I tried to imagine how this small vessel might have appeared as it was caught and battered by the unmerciful ravages of the storm that night. Becoming familiar with the ship and the accounts of her demise, I began to form pictures of her agony in my mind. Based on the data available, these imaginary visions resulted in a portrayal of the lightship and the following description of her. As the blowing tops of mountainous seas barely reflected the dreary first light of that cold November morning, contorted reflections from her ever faithful beacons danced sporadically on tormented waves. Tethered to her large mushroom anchor, her hull was yanked, then released, over and over again in torturous repetition by the convulsive and cruel sea action. Barricaded inside their tiny quarters, the crew, at first confident in the staunchness of their craft, undoubtedly began to grow fearful of the roaring storm and its unprecedented nature. That their boiler was lit and offering protected warmth to the end was small consolation for the men who were surely slammed about in the chaos.

Although the masters of several passing vessels did not see her usual welcome beacon, it was not certain the ship was lost until Tuesday morning, November 11, when a life buoy from the lightship and parts of railing or small doors were found on the shore inside the Buffalo breakwater. A search of the area near the lightship station was ordered with the lightship tender *Crocus* and the tug *Yale* as patrols scoured the beaches for other clues. Although the items picked up were definitely from *Lightship No. 82*, they did not prove the vessel was lost, for it was determined these items could have washed off the deck of the vessel. Soon, however, what was believed to be a drawer from the lightship's galley and a small sailboat from the ship were found, which all but verified the loss. The next day, the brass gasoline tank cover attached to a board from the ship's powerboat was found, indicating that both of the small boats from the lightship were mangled from the storm. Then came the shocking discovery of a note scrawled on a wooden hatch cover with the grim message "Goodbye Nellie. . .Ship is breaking up fast. . .Williams." The item was found on the beach by a local fisherman. Although Mrs. Williams stated her husband, Capt. Hugh McClennan Williams, did not refer to her as "Nellie," and though she did not believe the note was writ-

190

ten by him, she was still positive the message was from her husband. There was also the question of whether a husband would sign such a note to his wife with only his last name. Captain Williams may have figured by signing "Williams" that whoever found the message would positively connect it to the stricken ship. Regardless, if tragedy arose, Williams had promised to write his wife such a note. The ominous message and the dire circumstances that prevailed, however, did not sway the courageous Mrs. Williams. Not giving up hope, she spent two disheartening days aboard the lurching deck of the *Crocus*, searching the waters for her husband. Many years later, Mrs. Williams would say that she believed her husband, perhaps near death, was unable to write the mysterious note himself.

Having been in the water for almost a year after the loss of the ship, the body of Charles Butler, the chief engineer of *Lightship No. 82*, was discovered floating in the Niagara River at the foot of Ferry Street on the west side of Buffalo. Recognized by his heavy black sweater-coat, a gold cuff button, and a missing finger, his wife, who lived in the area, identified the remains, which were well preserved.

Despite several attempts to locate the hulk of the lightship that winter, not until the next May did the search vessel *Surveyor* discover the wreck in sixty-two feet of water two

191

miles from her station. Contrary to the belief that the crew was still inside the ship, divers found no trace of their bodies. Although the hull was intact, the heavily damaged wooden superstructure, with crushed lantern room, hatches, windows, and doors, gave profound testimony to the punishing forces and fury of the seas that found their way inside the supposedly staunch vessel. For $36,000, the Reid Wrecking and Towing Company raised the wreck on September 16, 1915. Unbelievably, the small but gallant ship, after going to its temporary grave, would see service again. Refitted at Detroit, she would have a long and honorable career until 1945, when she was finally scrapped.

19. THE BARGE *PLYMOUTH* AND THE TUG *MARTIN*

Did they abandon the *Plymouth* in the howling gale?
Who would believe the hard-hearted tale?
Did they actually leave without a good-bye?
Was the haunting note in the bottle a lie?

On Friday morning, November 7, 1913, the first of the two deadly 1913 storms was centered over northwestern Wisconsin. Had there been a satellite view of the system, it would have shown a storm that was well developed but not particularly strong. Barometric pressures were on the way down as a Canadian low pressure moved toward the Minnesota border. Ahead of the storm, winds remained in the teens to low twenties. Gradually, that same day, the system tracked eastward across Wisconsin as cold air behind an associated cold front began to surge southward. By 7:00 P.M., northwest winds at Duluth were clocked at sixty miles per hour, while Marquette had southeast winds with a temperature of fifty degrees. By now, the storm, which had not strengthened that much during the day, was centered between Rhinelander, Wisconsin, and Menominee, Michigan. During the early morning hours of the eighth, the storm, with cold air surging in behind it, was moving across northern Lake Michigan and getting stronger. At 7:00 A.M, the storm was positioned south of Pellston, Michigan. The winds were northwest at forty miles per hour at Marquette, while snow was falling over most of Wisconsin. During these morning hours, gale and storm-force northwest winds attacked Lake Michigan.

Practically in the center of the storm as it slammed across the northern reaches of the lake, the tug *James H. Martin*, with the barge *Plymouth* in tow, was at anchor in the lee of the protective coast off tiny St. Martin's Island. Sailing from Menominee and bound for Search Bay[37] for a load of lumber, Capt. Louis Setunsky, the recently employed skipper on the

193

The barge *Plymouth*. (Wisconsin Marine Historical Society)

Martin, was earlier plagued by strong southwest winds that continuously pushed his barge to starboard. Surrendering to the aggravating conditions, Setunsky hove to, deciding to wait out the storm. Having serious second thoughts about his new position, Setunsky felt slighted on discovering that the condition of his tug, now engulfed in the raging storm, was a far cry from what he was led to believe. In no uncertain terms, he was voicing this grievance to his employer and owner of the tug, Donald McKinnon, who was also aboard serving as the engineer. The forty-four-year-old, 62.8-foot wooden tug had seen better years. With their usual low freeboard[38], any tug would have problems in heavy sea conditions, but on top of this predicament, the hull of the *Martin* leaked profusely, and her engine was in poor shape, requiring constant, coaxing attention. Setunsky, frustrated with the mess he was in, stared out his cabin window at the *Plymouth*, which was now barely visible in the growing snowstorm.

One of the oldest wooden hulls still on the lakes, the fifty-nine-year-old barge *Plymouth* was near the end of her long career, too. Launched in March 1854, at Ohio City (Cleveland), Ohio, the 213-foot, 35-foot beam vessel, originally built as a combination package freight and passenger steamer for the Western Transit Company, was then the largest vessel on the lakes. Contradictions in the old records list her as a steamer and an unrigged barge from 1883 to 1885, as a steamer and schooner in 1886 and 1887, and as a barge from 1888 to 1913. On October 24, 1887, in a northeast gale, she was driven ashore on the north end of Presque Isle, at Marquette. Aground there all winter, she was rescued and became the property of the Reid Wrecking Company in 1888. Refitted with steel arches and a new bottom, she was sent back to work in 1889. Her home ports were listed as Buffalo

The barge *Plymouth* and tug *James H. Martin*

through 1887, Detroit in 1888, Port Huron from 1889 to 1902, Cleveland from 1903 to 1911, and Marquette from 1912 to 1913. The old and tired *Plymouth*, indeed, had "been around."

Entangled in rightful ownership litigation in 1913, she listed three different owners: the C. J. Hubel Company and the McKinnon & Scotte Company, both of Menominee, Michigan, and the Custom House of Milwaukee. This dispute was in fact the reason that Deputy United States Marshal Chris Keenan was aboard as a custodian. Not at all a sailor, his monotonous duty was to safeguard the interests of all the alleged owners by protecting the vessel against damage, mutiny, or piracy. So, you can bet that the accomplished master of the *Plymouth*, Axel Larsen, in command of the motley crew of six "greenhorns," which included Keenan, had his hands full as well.

In the blizzard, with temperatures dropping fast and the winds still increasing, the situation on the tug and barge looked increasingly bleak. But landsmen on both shores were also witnessing the ferocity and fury of the unusually strong storm. All cross-lake ferry traffic was canceled. Eighty-mile-per-hour winds were clocked at Muskegon where, intermixed with the blowing snow, there flew dangerous projectiles of storm-torn debris. At Holland, many boathouses were smashed, pleasure boats were sunk, and the shoreline interurban rails were undermined. Citizens at Milwaukee watched in disbelief as the thunderous surf tore away fifteen hundred feet of a brand-new breakwater and destroyed two nearby pile drivers. Two Chicago men were blown off their feet and flung to their deaths in the Chicago River. On the shoreline, thousands of curious gawkers

Believed to be a photograph of the early hull of the *Plymouth*. (Dossin Great Lakes Museum)

196

The *Plymouth* aground near
Marquette, Michigan, 1887.
(Milwaukee Public Library)

The *Plymouth* with rags still on her booms. (Dossin Great Lakes Museum)

Possibly the *Martin* was serving here as a fireboat. (Dossin Great Lakes Museum)

watched the schooner *C. E. Buys*, just a mile or so out on the lake, pleading for help as she flew her distress signals.

As the winds were now out of the north, Captain Setunsky decided to try again, feeling relieved knowing that at least he would not have to contend with the southwest wind that hampered his earlier advance. But the winds he headed into now were stronger, and once under way, he realized that the underpowered tug could hardly keep her tow in check, much less make headway in the heavy sea. Making hardly any progress, Setunsky, though there must have been heated discussions against the idea, decided to leave the *Plymouth* in St. *Martin*'s Passage off the lee of Gull Island. Although it was said that they blew signals for the barge to drop anchor and to signify their departure, those on the barge surely must have been frightfully shocked to see the tug sail off and leave them in the raging storm. It is questionable, too, whether they could even hear signals from the tug over the roaring wind. However, leaving a barge to fend for itself in a storm, although not a common practice, was not as heartless as it may have seemed. A barge with big anchors had a better-than-average chance to ride out a blow. An example of this occurred in the great storm of 1905 when the steamer *Mataafa*, towing the barge *Nasmyth*, could not enter Duluth Harbor. Cutting the barge loose several miles out, the *Mataafa* wound up broken on the outer piers, but the *Nasmyth* rode out the storm safely. And, in the same storm, unable to link up again after their towline had snapped, the steamer *James H. Prentice*, on the way to Gladstone,

Michigan, left the old barge *Halstead* on its own to wash up safely, though precariously, on the beach.

Standard practice in this case, however, appeared to be a very cruel action when Captain Setunsky returned to the scene many hours later to discover that the *Plymouth* had disappeared; he had gotten as far as Point Detour only twelve miles from the barge. Thinking that her anchor chains had parted and that he might find her somewhere down on the east shore of the lake, a thorough search by the *Martin* and other vessels was conducted, but the *Plymouth* had sunk with all seven lives. Because the home port of the tug was Menominee where most of the crew of the *Plymouth* crew hailed from, as could be expected, there was much criticism and resentment brewing in the small town over the incident. It was nothing in comparison, though, to the bitterness the townspeople displayed a week later when a note from Chris Keenan was found in a bottle on the beach near Pentwater, Michigan: "Dear Wife and Children: We were left up here, in Lake Michigan by McKinnon, captain of the James H. *Martin*; tug an anchor. He went away and never said good-bye or anything to us. Lost one man yesterday. We have been out in the storm forty hours. Goodbye dear ones. Might see you in heaven. Pray for me. Chris K. P. S. I felt so bad I had another man write for me. Goodbye forever."

Only two of the crew of the *Plymouth* were ever found. Chris Keenan's body came ashore at Onekama, Michigan, nearly eighty-three miles from Gull Island. About a month later, Capt. Axel Larsen's body was found north of Muskegon, some 120 miles from where the barge was last seen. At a hearing in Marquette, Michigan, government steamboat inspectors revoked McKinnon's license, but concluded that there was no criminal liability in the actions of either Captain Setunsky or owner-engineer Donald McKinnon. As if ashamed of her part in the sinister incident, the tug *James H. Martin* sank in Menominee Harbor on the last day of November 1913. According to Wisconsin diver Richard Bennett, the wreck of the *Plymouth* lies right side up in forty to fifty feet of water, five hundred yards off Poverty Island Lighthouse on a heading of 220 degrees. If Setunsky and McKinnon did know in their hearts that they wrongfully left their brother sailors in the terrible storm, they would most likely have been haunted by the note and the lost crew for the rest of their lives.

20. THE *ARGO* AND OTHER SURVIVORS

A few lucky ships fought through the blow.
And unless you were there you'd never know.
The frightful gale, the towering sea,
A freezing hell it had to be.

It is hard to comprehend how any vessel could withstand the storms that ravaged the Great Lakes from November 7 to 10, 1913. According to the March 1914 *Marine Review*, nineteen vessels were destroyed, of which thirteen sank with all hands and six were total constructive losses. Another twenty vessels were grounded or stranded. Many other vessels sailed through or near the worst areas of the storms. The masters of these ships recorded eyewitness accounts of their experiences and in many cases narrowly escaped the clutches of the "King of Storms." The following excerpts are from some of those accounts.

The 198-foot, single-screw steamer *Argo* was built at the Detroit Dry Dock Company in 1895 for the Argo Steamship Company of Cleveland, Ohio. Having only a 35-foot beam and five, 8 x 15-foot hatches, this little workhorse could carry 42,000 bushels of wheat or 819,000 board feet of lumber. Her red hull, white cabins, and slightly raked fore and mizzen masts gave her a trim yet hardy appearance. With a regular crew of fourteen, her season was usually spent hauling lumber from northern Michigan to the lower lake ports. As the 1913 shipping season was drawing to a close, the *Argo*, with the barge *George B. Owen* in tow, was anchored in Thunder Bay, off Alpena, Michigan. Master of the *Argo*, Capt. Winslow Randall, wrote about this experience in his personal log:

> Before dark I had crew try and fasten our deck load down as the wind was picking up the plank as though they were tooth picks. Then I strung a life line from foremast to mizzen mast so one could walk on top of deck load and have something to hang on to as it

The 198-foot steamer *Argo*.

was impossible to stand the wind without this line and all one could do to hang on. At 10:30 P.M. wheelsman reported he thought we were dragging or anchors. I could not believe it! Being familiar with bottom at that particular spot—4 fath [four fathoms] water three quarters of a mile off Whitefish Point—so called by fisherman.[39] Wind was then NNE and the average velocity of wind from 9 P.M. until 6 A.M. November 9th was 85 miles per hour. At 10:30 P.M. it was over 100 mph according to weatherman at Alpena, Michigan. We got under way night of November 9th and in the morning I drew a pail of water from Lake and let it settle and there was close to an inch of mud in bottom of pail—which shows how Lake Huron was stirred up. Getting down near St. Clair River I passed the Str *Price* bottom up—not knowing what had happened I figured it must be a Pig [pigboat or whaleback] turned turtle—it did not seem possible that a ship size of the *Price*, coal loaded, could over turn completely bottom up.

Captain Hagen, on the steamer *H. M. Hanna, Jr.*, about fifteen miles above Pointe Aux Barques, Lake Huron:

Tremendous seas were coming over our bow and our starboard quarter and over the whole vessel in fact, and the seas had carried away part of our after cabin and had broken in our pilot house window and had torn off the top of the pilot house.

Capt. P. A. Anderson of the steamer *Centurion*:

202

The *Argo*

The *Argo* with the barge *Mingo*.

We did not see Pointe Aux Barques, but we saw Harbor Beach for a few minutes and got our bearings. The barometer was registering 28.45 at 11:00 A.M. It was 2:01 P.M. on November 9th when we passed Fort Gratiot, and twenty minutes later I could not see the length of my own boat, the wind was blowing about sixty miles per hour from the north. Late afternoon on November 10, in the St. Clair Ship Canal, he reported, "My barometer that morning registered 28.35."[40]

Capt. Thomas J. Carney, on the steamer *H. W. Smith* off Harbor Beach:

At 3 P.M. [November. 9] the seas began to get so big that they broke in the pilot house doors and windows and forward cabins. At 6 P.M. we lost control of the ship and she began to go off in the trough of the sea. Then I immediately ordered her wheel hardover and after some difficulty we managed to head down the lake. Then the seas began to pile over the stern, breaking in the after cabins and washing rubbish down in the aft of the engine room. The engineer for a while had a hard time keeping the different pieces of framework from being washed into the engine.

Capt. W. C. Iler, on the steamer *George G. Crawford*, near Sanilac, Michigan, reported losing both anchors in a snowstorm with seventy-five to eighty-mile-per-hour winds about 1:10 A.M. Monday, November 10. Groping in the blinding snow for nearly twenty-six hours, he navigated by using his sounding machine, which he highly praised.

Capt. L. W. Watson on the steamer *George F. Brownell*:

The wind on Lake Huron from 9:30 A.M. to 7 P.M. November 9th varied from N. by E. to NE. by N. and at times from seventy to eighty mph. Clouds were traveling from north to south until 4:30 p.m. when they came from N N W. One effect of the high wind was that at times when a sea would strike the ship the spray would be blown as high as the headlight which was seventy-five feet above the water. At other times the velocity was such as to prevent the spray from rising over four or five feet. The temperature fell rapidly to a low point and the ship iced up fast. The seas appeared to follow each other closely in series of three which would strike with terrific force.

Capt. James B. Watts on the steamer *J. F. Durston* off Thunder Bay Island, Lake Huron:

At noon Sunday, November 9th it was blowing a hurricane from due north and it was freezing hard and snowing. Steering due north, the sea increasing all the time and our decks and hatches were coating up with ice. Our coal bunker was filled up with coal above the spar deck which helped to strengthen the cabins against the sea. I leave it to the coating of ice that we got on our hatches and around our forward cabins and windows, that we lived through the storm as well as we did.

Capt. S. A. Lyons, on the steamer *J. H. Sheadle* near Harbor Beach:

The bell rang for supper at 5:45 P.M., [November 9] when a gigantic sea mounted our stern, flooding the fantail, sending torrents of water through the passageways on each side of the cabin, concaving the cabin, breaking the windows in the after cabin. Volumes of water came down on the engine through the upper skylights and at times there were from 4 to 6 ft. of water in the cabin. It was blowing about 70 miles an hour at this time, with high seas, one wave following another very closely. Owing to the sudden force of the wind the seas had not lengthened out as they usually do when the wind increases in the ordinary way. In about four hours the wind had come up from 25 to 70 miles an hour. At 4:15 A.M., November 10th, I turned again, heading south, one-quarter west. The rolling was very bad I was lifted right off my feet. Only by the greatest effort were the second Mate and myself able to hold onto the stanchions on the top house, our legs being parallel with the deck most of the time. Again and again she plunged forward, only to be baffled in her attempts to run before it, sometimes fetching up standing and trembling from stem to stern. She was buffeted about by the tremendous seas, almost helpless, dipping her hatches in the water on either side. I never have seen seas form as they did at this time; they were large and seemed to run in series, one mounting the other like a mighty barrier.

Capt. J. A. Stewart, on the steamer *Presque Isle*, which was landlocked at Midland, Ontario, reported that he never saw the barometer so low—it was 28.50. Capt. F. A. West, on the steamer *William G. Mather*, having passed Whitefish Point, related, "The snow by this time was a blizzard—you could not look into it, and the wind was a continuous roar. We could not hear our own whistle forward."

Capt. F. D. Perew, on the steamer *Angeline*:

The *H. M. Hanna, Jr.*, on Port Austin Reef.

After quarters demolished.

All hatches stripped.

Another view of the *Hanna* on the rocks.

Showing where the
Hanna struck the
reef.

Smashed cabins
aft.

The owners' room
forward.

The Gallery.

The *L. C. Waldo*, with smashed cabins, grounded and broke in two off Gull Rock, Lake Superior. (Great Lakes Historical Society)

At 1:00 A.M., November 9th, the wind had shifted to about north and blew hard; we were then somewhere about twenty-five miles from Cove Island, entrance to Georgian Bay, making good weather of it. At about 2:00 A.M. the wind shifted to the southwest heavy, and that was when I noticed that our barometer went down below 28 and we expected to get a hurricane.

Capt. Charles Fox, on the steamer *Choctaw*:

We left the Soo at about 8:35 A.M., November 6th, bound for Marquette—the barometer being about 28.95 and still going down—expecting to stop at Whitefish. Before we reached Point Aux Pine the wind had shifted to the south and was blowing hard. We continued out past Whitefish with the wind still south—strong—and the barometer still going down. We kept the south shore close aboard and arrived at Marquette at 2:00 A.M., November 7th, with the wind southwest strong and the barometer about 28.50.

One of the most terror-filled stories about the ships on Lake Superior was that of the steamer *L. C. Waldo* loaded with ore for Cleveland out of Two Harbors in the early hours of November 8. Capt. John Duddleson and his second mate, fighting the storm and steering by their compass, were alarmed to hear the "rumbling sound" of a giant wave approaching their ship. This wave, larger than the others, lifted the stern of the vessel high into the air, smashed onto the decks, and carried away the pilothouse and forward cabins. Just before the onslaught, Duddleson and his mate

208

barely escaped being washed overboard by diving headlong into a hatchway. Their compass useless and their steering wheel damaged beyond use, it was impossible to keep the vessel headed into the wind. In sheer desperation, the wheelsman ventured aft on the deck awash with waves that were coming over his ice-covered footing to get to the lifeboat compass. With this compass, situated on a broken stool, they steered with the auxiliary wheel for four hours, by the light of a lantern. Steering in this manner, they came only a half-mile short of the passage between Gull Rock and Keweenaw Point, where they went aground on a reef off Gull Rock. Before their vessel broke in two, the crew of twenty-four gathered in the aft cabins, where for two days and nights they burned cabin furnishings in a bathtub to keep warm. Lifesaving teams from the Portage and Eagle harbor stations finally rescued the entire crew.

A statement in the March 1914 *Marine Review* offers the most unbelievable footnote of the disaster:

The history of such a storm, of course, can only be related by a recital of individual experiences. Probably no one who was out in it on Sunday November 9th, will ever forget it. The wind blew at Cleveland for one minute on Sunday (at 4:40 P.M.) at the rate of 79 miles per hour and was followed by a wind for nine hours thereafter varying from sixty to sixty-two miles an hour.

21. THE 1913 STORMS POEM

Turning turtle out on the lake,
Twenty-eight sailors she would take.
But what ship was it? How could this be?
'Twas the 1913 storms' biggest mystery.

Did they pull their brothers from the freezing sea?
Did they help them when they heard their plea?
Could that be why the poor souls washed ashore,
Wearing different life belts than they did before?

The brand-new ship came off the ways,
Her life was short, only numbered in days.
The strongest yet built, everyone knew.
But the "King of Storms" would take her too.

The salties are stronger, so they said,
Why, Cape Horn sailors come back from the dead!
They can take the high seas, for heaven's sakes,
But they never sailed the November lakes.

The engineer gave the lady his coat,
For his being saved was quite remote.
The captain's life preserver she also wore,
For another human, one could do no more.

Who knows what ghastly horrors prevailed,
During the freezing gale in which they sailed.
For they lashed themselves to the pitching craft,
Those three dead sailors on the *McGean* raft.

The *Hydrus* and *Argus*, the *Price* and the *Scott*,
Unlucky sister ships believe it or not.
Related by their particulars, the records show,
And they all were lost in the horrible blow.

A few bits of wreckage and one of her boats,
No poor souls in their water-soaked coats.
No word for sweethearts or waiting wives,
The *Scott* just vanished with twenty-eight lives.

Superior, they say, never gives up her dead.
Maybe she'll offer some wreckage instead.
She has no compassion, the legend is renowned.
So, consider it lucky when a body is found.

The *Leafield* and two sisters lost near Thunder Bay
Is one strange mystery, even to this day.
They all carried rails; they all were stout.
Just how it could be was never figured out.

Without permission to leave their place,
The ship was lost except for a trace.
They fought the storm as best could be.
And they gave their lives so others could see.

Did they abandon the *Plymouth* in the howling gale?
Who would believe the hard-hearted tale?
Did they actually leave without a good-bye?
Was the haunting note in the bottle a lie?

A few lucky ships fought through the blow.
And unless you were there you'd never know.
The frightful gale, the towering sea,
A freezing hell it had to be.

Notes

1. Other assistance included breaking out areas of ice to free supply traffic to various islands.
2. The *City of Alpena* was later renamed the *State of Ohio*.
3. The *City of Mackinac* was later renamed the *State of New York*.
4. The *City of Buffalo*, at 298. 3', was then the largest side-wheeler on the lakes.
5. The *Texas* was built in May 1912. Its length was 573' x 95' beam.
6. The USS *Wolverine* was previously called the USS *Michigan*.
7. IX-64 was the navy designation for this miscellaneous auxiliary vessel.
8. By comparison, the length of the flight deck of the USS *Enterprise* CV-6 was 809 feet. The CVE-Escort carrier flight decks were smaller, measuring 490 feet.
9. The records for 1945 appear to have been gleaned of all mishaps.
10. For the story of *Lightship No. 82*, see chapter 18.
11. The eastern Michigan shore on lower Lake Huron from Lexington to the mouth of the St. Clair River is considered exceedingly dangerous without the help of a lightship's beacon or other navigation aid.
12. The *Huron Lightship* had a light range of 14 miles, a fog-signal range of 2 miles, and a radar-reflector range of 15 miles.
13. At Erie, Pennsylvania, on November 9, 1913, a reading of 28.61" was registered. A reading of 28.51" was registered at Buffalo, March 25, 1947. Also at Buffalo, on January 26, 1978, a low reading of 28.41" was registered.
14. For the story of the *Argus*, formerly the *Louis Woodruff*, see chapter 12.
15. *Regina* is pronounced "reh JINE uh."
16. "Light," in ship terminology, means having ballast but no cargo.
17. In November 1966 strain gauges on the *Edward L. Ryerson*, which was sailing on Lake Michigan during the same storm that sank the *Daniel J. Morrell* on Lake Huron, recorded a stress of twenty-three thousand pounds per square inch—much more than had ever been recorded on any ocean vessel.
18. The sewer pipe was measured by divers to be sixteen inches in diameter.
19. This scene is portrayed in my painting of the *Regina*.
20. The *Charles Price* lies in about forty-five feet of water.
21. The two largest U.S. vessels then were the *James M. Schoonmaker* and the *William P. Snyder*, both 597 feet long.
22. As of this writing, five of the eight vessels lost on Lake Huron have been found. All lying upside down, they offer strong evidence that they all capsized. These are the *Argus, John McGean, Charles Price, Regina*, and *Isaac M. Scott*.
23. Point Clark is almost due east of Port Austin on the Canadian shore of Lake Huron about twenty-five miles above Goderich, Ontario.
24. Many accounts state that the *Wexford* was carrying rails, but close to

where her victims and wreckage came ashore it was reported that the beach was white with grain.

25. This supports the two-storm theory. The first storm was forecast on the twenty-four-hour weather advisory. After the first storm passed, mariners believed all was well and ventured out to be caught in the second, unforecast, giant.

26. "To wet the galley tables" refers to wetting the galley tablecloths to keep things from sliding off the tables in rough seas.

27. In recent years, when the Erie Sand and Steamship Company of Erie, Pennsylvania, acquired the *Richard J. Reiss*, the new owners painted out the middle initial *J* on the sides of the ship as a precaution against any unlucky fate.

28. For the stories of these ships, see chapter 17.

29. Capt. S. A. Lyons, on the steamer *J. H. Sheadle*, several times turned his vessel into the wind and back down the lake before the storm, in desperate attempts to weather the storm.

30. Not shown on the newer charts, Mamaimse Point would be near Montreal River, Ontario.

31. The *Paliki* apparently escaped an unlucky fate by being sold off the lakes in 1916. Renamed the *Carmella*, she was scrapped in 1930.

32. The well deck is the space on the main deck of a steamer between the topgallant forecastle and the cabins amidships or between the mid-ship cabins and the topgallant poop or both.

33. Angus Island is about the size of a football field and is 4 miles south of Cape Thunder on a bearing of 215 degrees.

34. CPO Robert King of the Canadian Coast Guard Search and Rescue station in Thunder Bay has recently visited the lighthouse tower on Angus Island and states that on a clear day you can see parts of a wreck that is believed to be the *Monkshaven*.

35. In 1893, *LV-37*, in relief of the lightship at Five Fathom Bank off New Jersey, sank with the loss of four of her six-man crew.

36. These were rounded, cigar-shaped ships built by Alexander McDougall from 1888 to 1898.

37. Search Bay is in the Straits of Mackinac, north of Bois Blanc Island on the southern shore of the Upper Peninsula of Michigan.

38. Freeboard is the height of the side of the hull from waterline to upper deck or rail.

39. Here Randall is referring to Whitefish Point on the north shore of Thunder Bay, near Alpena, Michigan.

40. One of the lowest barometric pressures ever recorded over North American land mass—28.61''—was officially registered at Erie, Pennsylvania, November 9, 1913.

Bibliography

Alden, Cmdr. John D. "When Airpower Rode on Paddle Wheels." *Inland Seas* (Summer 1962): 119-22.

"*Aquarama* in New Role." *Detroit News*, June 26, 1955.

"*Aquarama* Makes Illegal Entry at Windsor." *Detroit Free Press*, August 23, 1956.

"*Aquarama* Protected by Radar. " *Cleveland Plain Dealer*, July 29, 1956.

"*Aquarama* Slashes Windsor Seawall." *Detroit Free Press*, Aug. 23, 1956.

"*Aquarama* Wake Spills 2 Small Boats; 9 Safe." *Detroit News*, July 15, 1957.

Barcus, Frank. *Freshwater Fury*. Detroit: Wayne State University Press, 1960.

Barry, James P. "*Ships of the Great Lakes: Three Hundred Years of Navigation.*" California: Howell-North Books, 1973.

Beck, Horace. *Folklore and the Sea*. Middletown, Conn.: Wesleyan University Press, 1973.

"Bee-Ohs Gone, Whee-OO-OP Is Now in Charge." *Port Huron Times Herald*, Aug. 20, 1970.

"Behind the Waterfront." *Cleveland Plain Dealer*, Nov. 25, 1955.

"Blue Water Portrait: Aboard the *Mackinaw*." *Port Huron Times Herald*, April 22, 1984.

"Boat Is *Price*." *Port Huron Times Herald*, Nov. 15, 1913.

"Boat Launched at Lorain." *Lorain Journal* [Lorain, Ohio], Aug. 5, 1903.

Boyer, Dwight. *True Tales of the Great Lakes*. New York: Dodd Mead & Company, 1971.

Brabander, Capt. Bob. Interview with James Clary, Dec. 1985.

Brockel, Harry C. "World War II Secrets of Lake Michigan." *Inland Seas* (Summer 1978): 103–12.

"Bugs Delay New Lakes Giant." *Detroit News*, Nov. 3. 1971.

"Carruthers Docked for Repair." *Collingwood Enterprise* [Collingwood, Ont.], June 26, 1913.

"Castro Kept Her on Lakes." *Detroit Free Press*, June 25, 1962.

Colwell, Lt. Cmdr. Keith. Interview with James Clary, May 20, 1991.

"Convert Ship to Luxury Craft at Dock." *News Palladium* [Benton Harbor, Mich.], June 16, 1955.

Craig, John. *The Noronic Is Burning*. Don Mills, Ont: General Publishing Co., 1976.

Davenport, Don. "The Great Storm of 1913." *Great Lakes Travel and Living*, Dec. 1988, 12-17.

"Deep Secret Lake Puzzle Unraveled." *Milwaukee Journal*, Nov. 2, 1976.

"Diver Revives Watery Mystery." *Detroit Free Press*, July 21, 1963.

"Dry Dock Company Provide Royal Good Time for Visitors to Twin Cities from Winnipeg." *Fort William Times Journal* [Thunder Bay, Ont.], June 2, 1913.

Eldridge, R. A. "Chick." Interview with James Clary, Sept. 8, 1988.

_____. "Do You Remember? USS *Sable* (IX-81) USS *Wolverine* (IX-64)." *Approach*, Feb. 1979.

"Erie Yard Uses Newest Shipbuilding Techniques." *Lake Carriers Bulletin*, Sept. Oct., 1969.

"Fastest Passenger Vessel on the Lakes Goes to Sea." *Detroit News*, June 3, 1956.

"Fear 5 More Boats with 106 Men Lost." *Cleveland Leader*, Nov. 14, 1913.

Garrett, BM2 Bill. Interview with James Clary, May 18, 1983.

Gillham, Skip. "Sadly We Remember the *Noronic*." *Telescope*, Nov.-Dec. 1974.

Great Lakes Marine News. *Cleveland Plain Dealer*, July 23, 1955.

_____. *Cleveland Plain Dealer*, April 4, 1953.

Greenwood, John O. *Namesakes 1910-1919*. Cleveland: Freshwater Press, 1986.

Havighurst, Walter. *The Great Lakes Reader*. London: Collier-Macmillan, 1966.

"History of the Great Lakes." Chicago: J. H. Beers & Company, 1899.

"Holiday Marks Occasion of Launching." *Lorain Journal* [Lorain, Ohio], Feb. 23, 1908.

Honke, Capt. F. J. Interview with James Clary, June 10, 1983.

"Huron Is Here." *Port Huron Times Herald*, June 6, 1971.

"It's Great to Be a Shipbuilder." *American Shipbuilder*, May 1949.

"Just a Breeze." *Detroit Free Press*, March 30, 1947.

Kanaby, Edward. Interview with James Clary, October 19, 1988.

"Lake Cruises to Resume." *Detroit Free Press*, Sept. 27, 1954.

"Lake Ship *Aquarama* Opens Cruises Here." *Detroit News*, June 21, 1956.

Larson, Phil, and Schmidt, Paul. "*Regina* Yields Her Secrets." *Great Lakes Travel and Leisure*, Dec. 1988, 18-23.

"Launching under Ideal Conditions." *Lorain Journal* [Lorain, Ohio], June 12, 1909.

"Lightship's Final Trip a Memorable One." *Port Huron Times Herald*, June 13, 1971.

"Luxury Ship Almost Goes Ashore." *Detroit Times*, Aug. 26, 1956.

Manley, Capt. John J. "Great Lakes Lady Bares Her Fangs." *Inland Seas* (Spring 1958): 58 60.

Marcolin, Dr. Lorenzo. *Inland Seas*, 1965, 345-47.

Miller, Duane Ernest. "Aircraft Carriers on Lake Michigan." *Naval History Magazine* (Winter 1988): 42–43.

"Mishap at Launching." *Detroit Free Press*, Feb. 23, 1908.

"Monuments at Goderich and Kincardine." *Inland Seas* (Spring 1980): 20 21.

Murphy, Patrick. "The Loss of Lightship No. 82." *Telescope*, Jan.–Feb. 1975, 16–21.

Murray, Atholl. Interview with James Clary, May 20, 1991.

"Mystery of U.S. *Lightship No. 82*." *Manistee News Advocate* [Manistee, Mich.], Sept. 29, 1979.

"New Sound Heard on Great Lakes." *Detroit Free Press*, July 14, 1958.

"November Shipping Disasters." *Inland Seas* (Fall 1955): 221–22.

O'Carroll, Jim. Interview with James Clary, Nov. 1985.

"Old Lightship Does Double Duty." *Lambton Ontario Free Press*, Sept. 7, 1957.

"Old-Bee-Oh Is Last Great Lakes Lightship." *Detroit News*, Nov. 4, 1959.

Peters, Scott M. "The Gales of November 1913." *Michigan History*, 11-16.

Presley, John O. Interview with James Clary, Nov. 3, 1985.

Race, Richard. Interview with James Clary, March 21, 1991.

"Report Lightship Sinks with 6." *Buffalo Evening News*, Nov. 11, 1913.

Report of the United States Life-Saving Service 1899, 11-17.

Roland, Adm. (Ret.) Edwin. Interview with James Clary, June 9, 1983.

Schmidt, Paul J. "Found: The Wreck of the S.S. *Regina*." *Inland Seas* (Summer 1987): 82-93.

Schmidtman, Adm. (Ret.) Richard. Interview with James Clary, Dec. 15, 1983.

Schumacher, Capt. (Ret.) Gilbert F. Interview with James Clary, June 1, 1983.

Scott, George. *Scott's New Coast Pilot*. Detroit: The Free Press Printing Company, 1896.

"Steamer *Price* Now Disappeared from View." *Port Huron Times Herald*, Nov. 17, 1913.

"*Stewart J. Cort*—A Lot of Floating Lots." *Detroit Free Press*, April 9, 1972.

"*Stewart J. Cort* Handled Superbly in Sea Trials." *Lake Carriers Bulletin*, Sept.-Oct. 1971.

Stobbe, Donald. Interview with James Clary, Nov. 1985.

Stonehouse, Frederick. *Great Wrecks of the Great Lake*. Marquette, Mich.: Harbor Press, 1973.

"Str. Turns Turtle in Lake." *Port Huron Times Herald*, Nov. 11, 1913.

"Stubby Ship Grows Up." *Port Huron Times Herald*, April 9, 1972.

"Super Ship Being Built for Lake." *Detroit Free Press*, May 1, 1969.

Sykora, T. A. "1972 a New Era in Great Lakes Transportation." *Inland Seas*, 1972, 131–33.

"The 1913 Storm Once Again." *Inland Seas* (Fall 1971): 194–211.

"The *Aquarama*—Day Liner Deluxe." *Marine Engineering and Shipping Review*, Oct. 1955, 39-45.

"The Great Lakes Storm of November 7-10, 1913." *Beeson's Marine Directory*, 1914.

"The Greatest Storm in Lake History." *Marine Review*, March 1914, 1–24.

"The Largest Sidewheeler in the World, Steamer *Seeandbee*." *Marine Review*, Nov. 1912.

"Thousands Get Look at *Cort*." *Detroit News*, May 3, 1972.

"Thousands Greet Lake Giant." *Port Huron Times Herald*, May 3, 1972.

"Thousands Ogle Supership." *Detroit Free Press*, May 3, 1972.

"Toledo Shipyard Launches Another but the Most Powerful Icebreaker on the Great Lakes." *Great Lakes News*, March 1944, 6.

Trotter, David. "The Discovery of the *John McGean*." *Telescope*, Jan.–Feb. 1989, 3-8.

"Twelve Hundred Take Sunday Cruise." *Port Huron Times Herald*, June 21, 1963.

"Two Michigan Towns Fight Over Old Ship." *Detroit News*, Nov. 29, 1970.

"Two New Boats, Launchings, Yesterday at Buffalo and Lorain." *Detroit Free Press*, Sept. 13, 1903.

Van der Linden, Rev. Peter J. *Great Lakes Ships We Remember II*. Cleveland: Freshwater Press, 1984.

"Vessels Overwhelmed by Seas." *Collingwood Bulletin* [Collingwood, Ont.], Nov. 20, 1913.

Vogel, Michael, and Redding, Paul F. "Light Vessel 82." *Maritime Buffalo*, 67-72.

Vogel, Mike. "The Loss of *Light Vessel 82*." *Keeper's Log* (Summer 1989): 14-19.

"Wave Damage Boats, Docks." *Port Huron Times Herald*, June 20, 1957.

Witteman, Paul. "American Scene: On the Lakes Crushing Ice." *Time*, March 19, 1979.

"*Woodruff* Launched." *Detroit Free Press*, Aug. 6, 1903.

Yates, Ralph. Interview with James Clary, Aug. 23, 1984.

Zillmer, A. T. "History of Cleveland & Buffalo Transit Company C & B Line," Part 2. *Inland Seas* (Oct. 1945): 257-65.

_____. "History of Cleveland & Buffalo Transit Company C & B Line," Part 1. *Inland Seas* (Jan. 1945): 75-80.

_____. "The Great Ship *Seeandbee*." *Inland Seas* (Winter 1957): 283-87.

Zimmer, Nelson. Interview with James Clary, May 20, 1983.

Index